LAYER YOUR NOVEL

The Innovative Method for Plotting Your Scenes

By C. S. Lakin

The Writer's Toolbox Series

Layer Your Novel: The Innovative Method for Plotting Your Scenes

ISBN-10: 0-9861347-4-0

ISBN-13: 978-0-9861347-4-6

UBIQUITOUS PRESS

Morgan Hill, California

The Writer's Toolbox Series

Other Nonfiction Books by C. S. Lakin
The Writer's Toolbox Series

Writing the Heart of Your Story: The Secret to Crafting an Unforgettable Novel

Shoot Your Novel: Cinematic Techniques to Supercharge Your Writing

The 12 Key Pillars of Novel Construction: Your Blueprint for Building a Solid Story

The 12 Key Pillars Workbook

5 Editors Tackle the 12 Fatal Flaws of Fiction Writing

Say What? The Fiction Writer's Handy Guide to Grammar, Punctuation, and Word Usage

Crank It Out! The Surefire Way to Become a Super-Productive Writer

Other Books

Manipulating the Clock: How Fiction Writers Can Tweak the Perception of Time

Strategic Planning for Writers: 4 Easy Steps to Success

Table of Contents

Introduction: How Layering Brings Order out of Chaos

I've been writing novels and teaching novel structure for many years, but I've shied away from delving deep into what scenes should come where in a novel.

Why? Because there are countless books and blog posts that cover story structure, and a lot of great ones too, so, I figured, why should I add my two cents to the mix?

But the longer I thought about it, the more I realized I have some unique approaches and twists to the age-old question: "How do I write a great novel?"

The simple answer: by layering scenes—that's how.

I searched through titles and descriptions of dozens of writing craft books specific to structuring novels, and it hit me. None of these books talk about layering.

And I'll tell you why that confused me: layering is the most logical and intuitive way to structure a great story.

That's how I write all my novels. And the process isn't hard.

Creating Order out of Chaos

Novels are made up of scenes. Lots of scenes. If you're a pantser, you wing it and write whatever scenes come into your head. If you're a plotter, you sit down and make a list of as many scenes as you can think of, and then you try to put them in order as best you can, maybe create an outline, and then hope it works.

If you've written a lot of novels, you probably have a good sense where scenes need to fall in your story. You may know that you need some initial disturbance (also called "the Inciting Incident") to kick off your story somewhere near the beginning of your novel. And you might also know that at some point your protagonist should be pursuing a goal (but, believe me, a lot of writers don't even understand this is at the crux of plot and premise—and we'll see a couple of examples of this in current best sellers in Part 2 of this book) that builds to a climax somewhere near the end. And then you figure you need to wrap things up and end the darn thing.

How Many Scenes Do You Really Need to Start Writing?

Elizabeth George, in her terrific craft book *Write Away*, talks about how a writer should have about ten to fifteen scenes figured out before starting in on writing. That's going to vary from writer to writer. Some writers, like me, want to have about thirty to fifty scenes roughly figured out (and put on index cards) before diving in.

I always allow for spontaneous character takeover. Meaning, my characters—as is the norm with most well-developed characters— often go cavorting off in some direction I hadn't planned, ignoring my admonitions. And most of the time they know what they're doing, and I go along for the ride.

It's important to be flexible, to allow for new scene ideas to pop up. But I'm a stickler for strong structure. So whether you can pull a great novel together by laying out only a dozen key scenes before you start writing, or you need to work up more scenes, know that it's going to be a tremendous help if you do this "laying out" work before you start writing.

Stop "Pantsing" Already!

You pantsers out there: I don't know how you are still following my blog and reading yet another of my writing craft books (she says, laughing). You know how opposed I am to winging it when it comes to writing a novel.

Seriously, you writers who just "can't plot"—you can. You just don't want to.

2

And maybe you love to suffer through wasted months or years of your life throwing out draft after draft and agonizing all the way through (what is supposed to be a fun process!) your novel writing, wondering if your story is any good.

So I'm inviting you all—pantsers too—to try these pants on, this layering concept I'm presenting. You will find it so much more fulfilling to have efficient and productive writing time, which will give you more time for other things in life. Go on trips with your family. Watch the NBA finals. Take hikes with your dog. Smell the roses. You get to do all that with all the time you save when you plot instead of write by the seat of your pants.

Yes, It Is All about Structure

Maybe you've heard of plot points and turning points and pinch points, and you've resisted learning about them. I did. For years. I didn't want to write formulaic novels; I wanted to be original, different, unique.

I totally missed the boat on that one. I didn't get that I must follow expected novel structure, very specifically, to craft a terrific novel. I didn't get that there are specific types of scenes that must appear at specific places (percentage-wise) in my novel—or else! In other words, I thought I could just intuitively write my novels, and all the scenes would magically fall into the right slots and I could call it good.

Not.

And this applies to all genres, not just "genre" or popular fiction.

Here's the thing: if you want to sell well, you'll have a better chance if you stick with time-tested structure. And that means *understanding* what types of scenes you need to frame your novel and *where* to put them.

Ever wonder why some authors who sell millions of copies of their books struggle painfully with writing novel after novel, figuratively tearing their hair out and agonizing over each one? I know authors like this. They have a big love-hate relationship with writing. The "hate" part could be avoided though—this I truly believe. Because the "hate" part is due to their resistance to learn and master novel structure. In particular I'm talking about what scenes are needed where in a novel.

I don't know any writers (though I'm hoping they're out there) who, before starting to write their novel, sit down and work out their key scenes—well, other than my clients, who've taken my advice!

I'm talking about those milestones in your plot—which I refer to as the ten key scenes. Writers often lay out a list of a dozen or so scenes they want in their story, but they aren't thinking about *specific key scenes* that must go in *specific places*.

Framing Your Story

Do you do this? Maybe you have an idea how your novel will start. You might also picture the climax scene and the ending. Then, you possibly have some great ideas for scenes showing conflict or some plot complications. But this isn't the same as starting with a list of needed scenes and brainstorming to design those scenes to frame your story.

Framing is everything.

I often liken writing a novel to building a house. If you want a sturdy, well-built house, you can't just cut a bunch of neat-looking two-by-sixes and start hammering. You need a strong framework built on a solid foundation. Once you have that, you can proceed to the next tasks, like running electrical and nailing siding.

I go into great depth in my book *The 12 Key Pillars of Novel Construction* to show writers what the major novel components are and how to build them. But that's not what we're talking about here—at least not directly. What we're going to look at in this book, as a perfect companion to my pillars book, is the body of your scenes and how to puzzle-piece them together the best way—by layering.

In fact, you could liken the house-building process to a series of layers. First layer is the foundation and all that requires. Next layer is the frame-up—building the stud walls and framing the window areas and doors. And so on.

I've done a lot of stud-cutting and framing houses with my contractor husband, and I can say that building a house is akin to layering, one layer at a time. You can't put the roofing material on a house that hasn't been sided yet and doesn't have roof trusses. Ain't gonna happen. Everything goes in at the right time and in the right place.

Why should novel construction—or building anything, for that matter—be any different?

Get into the Layering Frame of Mind

So, the sooner you start thinking of building your novel in a layered way like that, the sooner this daunting task of novel-writing will become easier. Maybe not easy—because novels are highly complex animals. But why not make the effort as streamlined and approachable as possible?

This book you're reading presents a new and simple approach to grasping and mastering novel structure. I may possibly blast a few things you've been taught into smithereens. I'm hoping to rattle your cage a little and get you thinking in some new ways.

I see too many stuck writers. They have a head full of great scene ideas for their novel but just can't figure out what to do with them. They lay out their scenes as randomly as a person might shuffle a deck of cards and then throw all the cards onto the table, scoop them into their arms, and call it good.

It's not good. It's a disaster.

I use this specific layering method now for all my novels. I start with the premise and one-sentence story concept, which we'll go over. From there I get those ten key scenes figured out. After that, I start layering the next level of scenes. In this book, you'll see different ways you can layer, but this method, in general, works for any and all genres.

The purpose of using a "staged" or multilevel process is to help you flesh out that basic story idea you have and build a solid story. If you use this method in conjunction with building your twelve key pillars (your novel's individual components or "building materials" as detailed in *The 12 Key Pillars of Novel Construction*), you will have the blueprint you need to write a great novel.

Having a step-by-step instruction guide to building a novel is something I wish I'd had thirty years ago when I was biting off every nail trying to figure out this crazy business of writing fiction. I'm hoping, with this book, and the other books in my Writer's Toolbox Series, you won't needlessly suffer as I did.

Writers who've been using my Ten Key Scene Chart and referencing all my blog posts on this layering topic have been raving about this method, so I've gone ahead and pulled all my blog posts together, along with much additional material, and created this book. I'm confident you too will benefit greatly from layering your scenes.

Is the Jar Full Yet?

Have you ever seen anyone fill a jar with rocks and ask, "Is the jar full now?" Teachers love to do this with their young students. The students say yes, it's full, but then the teacher pours in pebbles, which fill in the spaces between the rocks. "Is it full yet?" the teacher asks.

And on it goes. After the pebbles, sand is poured in, to fill the tiniest spaces yet. But the jar isn't full! The last element added is water. And once water somehow finds space and fills to the brim, the jar is now declared full.

Think about your novel that way. If you put in sand first, there won't be room for the big rocks. And if you put in water before the sand, the water is going to be forced out and will overflow the brim once the sand gets poured in.

These first ten scenes are the big rocks. If you make them the right size, all ten will fit perfectly into your jar. The next ten scenes comprise the small pebbles. And the next ten . . . well, you get it.

Put too many useless scenes in your novel and the story will spill over the edges and ruin your nice new wood flooring. Put in all the cool minor scenes first (pebbles) and you might not have room for the rocks unless you take out a bunch of pebbles. And that's wasted effort (and may requiring dumping everything out and starting over again).

You don't have to layer in groups of ten—this isn't a rule. But I feel ten is a nice round number, and so this layering method will show you how to layer in groups of ten scenes. However, the additional layers you add may be made up of five scenes or fifteen. Find what works for you. Tweak the charts I provide in this book to fit your story's needs.

I hope this layering concept makes sense to you. I hope you'll give it a try.

But before we get to the actual layering process, we need to bust a few myths about structure.

Part 1: Story Framework

Chapter 1: Understanding Basic Story Structure

To put it simply, stories basically consist of a beginning, middle, and end. And because of this simple structure, some writing instructors rally in defense of the three-act structure. Meaning, since stories have a beginning, middle, and end, that must imply there are three acts.

Some claim Aristotle invented the three-act structure, but there is no truth to that. He only referred to those three parts to a story. You can use Aristotle's concept and translate your idea into three acts, if you like. What is the first act? How the story begins. What is the second act? The middle of the story (which includes the main crisis of the dominant plot). The third act is the climax of the story and the resolution. Okay, it's simplistic, but that's how many people justify the use of the three-act structure.

But framing a novel based on three acts as a matter of rule makes no sense to me. And I'll explain why.

And all this leads to the question: If we aren't going to look at stories as three-act constructs, what's the alternative?

Think in Terms of Problem and Solution

In my opinion, it makes much more sense when you're creating a story to think in terms of the natural structure of a problem. You have two main parts: the action that created it and the action that will resolve it.

The action that creates the problem is called the *Inciting Incident* or *initial disturbance*, and the action that resolves the problem is called the *principal action*. You have a threat, which is the driving force of the inciting action—a bad guy or bomb or zombie—and that's the cause of the problem. The anti-threat, which is the driving force of the principal action, is your protagonist or hero, the one who opposes the threat and solves the problem.

In *Harry Potter*, Voldemort is the threat that creates the problem. He is also the main source of the complications and crises, as well as the need for climactic actions to resolve the crises whenever Harry attempts to solve the problems Voldemort creates.

In *The Silence of the Lambs*, Buffalo Bill is the threat that causes the problem and also the main source of resistance when Clarice Starling tries to track him down.

In *The Lord of the Rings*, Sauron is the threat that is causing the problem and also the main source of resistance that creates the complications and crises when Frodo and his group try to solve the problem by destroying the ring of power.

After a story is created, of course, you can divide the action into any number of acts or parts that you like, but it's counterproductive to think in those terms at the story's inception. In other words, you shouldn't be using *act* structure to lay out or create the story.

How much better to focus on the natural structures surrounding the problem, which is the central event and heart of your story.

A Look at the Three-Act Structure

Since it seems logical to have three acts—to compartmentalize the beginning, middle, and end of your story—shouldn't you default to that? Simply, no.

In fact, the three-act structure so highly touted by many might just leave you aggravated.

Some structure methods work well for some people. Others just can't seem to fit their "square" story into a round hole. And there is no one perfect method. You may find that your novel doesn't break down well into three acts or two major plot or pinch points.

Here's another fact: just because you're using structure and following a framework for your story, it doesn't restrict you like a pulled-too-tight corset. We writers want the freedom of creativity, and a good framework should not be like the proverbial cage in which a bird might unfold its wings but cannot fly (a nod to Kahlil Gibran here).

So, while we need framework to hold up our story, we shouldn't be so neurotic or legalistic to the point of suffocating both our great story concept and our creative expression.

I personally don't lay out my novels noting where every one of these points go within a three-act structure. I rarely think in terms of "acts." When I step back and look at some of my novels, I see that I'd let the story line determine the number of acts and sections.

The Lowdown on the Three-Act Structure

So what's this three-act structure stuff all about, and is it a formula you should try? Or maybe start with and veer off from as needed?

The three-act structure has been around a long time. Screenwriters rely heavily on it, but it's not found in myths, legends, or other great stories of the past. Breaking stories up into acts is really an arbitrary choice.

Some research claims it originated with theater and television's need to have breaks in the programming. Sponsors have to plug their products via commercials, right?

I remember all the hundreds of scripts my mother wrote for TV (daytime soaps, nighttime series, etc.). Every single script had a scene "fade out" on specific pages (page ten, page twenty, or the like) for that purpose. It wasn't a choice; she had to structure her scripts that way to allow for the requisite commercials.

If you write a movie for television, it will likely have seven acts. Why? Because it has to allow for seven commercial breaks. And you will be expected to insert something intriguing at the end of each act to lure the audience back after the break. But that has nothing to do with story structure.

The Greeks had no act structure in their plays. The plays had one act. The Romans had five acts. It's arbitrary. Acts and their endings appeared in plays because of the need to have intermissions. People can't sit for three hours in a theatre without taking a break or going to the restroom. Sponsors (those companies that pay to promote their products during commercial breaks) want to sell something to target audiences. Networks need money and so have to cater to sponsors. None of this has anything to do with story.

So why should novelists blindly follow the herd? No reason.

Breaking Up Your Story into Large Chunks

So, the better way to look at a story, when you are creating one, is not to succumb to an arbitrary dividing into acts but to examine just what story you are telling and what might be the best way to break that story apart into chunks.

Well, why do you even need to do that—break it up? Because it helps you see the primary sections of your story so that you can set things up and build to those key plot developments, as well as create resolutions to these developments.

It doesn't have to be complicated. You don't have to break things up if you don't want to. But you might want to give it a try.

I love Michael Hauge's six-act story structure, and I often use that. Why? Because to me it's the most natural and intuitive. (You can learn more about his structure here on his website).

Let me share some brief examples of what I did in some of my novels.

In *A Thin Film of Lies*, one of my psychological mysteries, I have **Part One: Opening Shots**. This is a prologue, and it has a brief visual of the car accident that kills Libby Denham. This sets up the story, which is about the investigation into her death. These section breaks are told in the voice of the nemesis, although you don't learn who this character is until close to the end of the novel.

One-fifth in, you come to **Part Two: Developing in the Dark**. This section break has two paragraphs, using my camera/film motif to compare crime investigation with photography. The first section ends with Mike Jepson being interrogated about the hit-and-run, his life starting to unravel.

At about three-fifths into the novel, you come to **Part Three: Exposing the Negative**. Here I have just one paragraph about how powerful a camera is, and how a shot can destroy a life or even a nation. Part Two ends with Jepson arrested, and Part Three begins with him in jail, wondering how in the world this could have happened to him.

Part Four comes a bit past the four-fifths mark. I don't place these sections in based on exact location or page number, which is what some writing instructors advocate. I place these where they best fit and for specific reasons (which I'll further on). Part Four is called **"Fixing the Final Image"** and comprises only one brief paragraph that ties in with the title of the novel and pounds home the photography motif:

> *Just what is a piece of photographic paper, anyway? A flat piece of paper, coated with a minute amount of silver. In the blink of a shutter, a photographer can create reality or destroy lives. With that kind of power, what is this silver worth by the ounce? What would someone pay, and pay dearly, for that thin film of silver? Especially if it's a thin film of lies.*

I use this section break to set up the highly charged climax as Mike learns who his nemesis is and now has to find and stop that person before someone is killed.

Then I have an **Epilogue** called **"Parting Shots"** four pages before the end of the book. This last scene matches the style of the prologue, which are both told in the nemesis's voice (and readers now know who that character is).

I love bookending my novels so that the first and last scenes match in many ways (I'll show you another example of that later). The prologue scene in Part One shows the car accident that killed Libby. The Epilogue scene shows another person hit by another car and killed. Perfect bookends, and a way to end on a strong visual note.

The Basics You Really Need to Know

So, did I lay out my novel first into these six sections? Not at all. I first developed my story and followed the loose structure that included these basics (and which I lay out for you in *The 12 Key Pillars of Novel Construction Workbook*):

- *Opening situation that showcases the protagonist in her ordinary world.* In this case, my protagonist, Detective Fran Anders, has been called to the scene of the hit-and-run. Thus begins the investigation.

- *Inciting Incident that pushes the protagonist in a new direction.* Fran's initial look at the scene leads her to Mike Jepson as the primary suspect.

- *Goal set for the protagonist at around the 25% mark.* Fran now has to determine and prove that Jepson is guilty of this crime, but it's not as easy as it looks.

This is one of those standard novel structure benchmarks I wholly believe in. The protagonist must settle on a goal for the novel, and it's about at this juncture that the goal is set.

What you'll be soon learning is that these three scene types are part of the ten key scenes that make up your first layer.

* * *

Your assignment: Think about the natural structure of your story's "problem." You have two main parts: the action that created it and the action that will resolve it.

The action that creates the problem is called the *Inciting Incident* or *initial disturbance*, and the action that resolves the problem is called the *principal action*. Write a paragraph describing your story, identifying these two parts.

Now, think about your overall story, whether you've written any chapters or not. Do you see any natural sections in your plot? Play around with various numbers of acts, maybe even putting all your scenes on index cards and laying them out on a table so that you can create rows for acts. See what feels best for your particular story. You might find the exercise insightful and inspiring!

Chapter 2: A General Overview of Novel Framework

It's so important to understand that most novels (except epic stories that cover decades, such as a biography or family saga) are about a character going after one short-term goal.

Being clear about your protagonist's goal is paramount when it comes to structuring your novel. Why? Because without that goal as the heart of your premise, your story will be flawed. You need to build everything around the goal. This is true for movies and plays and novels.

Once you've figured out where to start your novel, based on that Inciting Incident at the start of your story, you then have these other sections:

- *The 25-50% section is the "Progress."* This is where the protagonist makes progress toward his goal. Many screenplays follow this specifically, to the second, and most movies do well sticking to this very expected formulaic structure. But I don't feel you have to force novels into this framework so fanatically. Novels really are different beasts than films and can succeed with creative or flexible structure, so don't get your shirt all bunched up trying to force your story into that round hole if it's got some sharp edges.

- *The 50-75% section presents bigger and bigger complications and obstacles* as you approach the *climax*, which falls anywhere between the *75%-99% region*. Again, it depends on the story. Hauge uses the movie *Thelma and Louise* as an example of a climax coming right at the very end of the story (the 100% mark). Really, how can you add any scenes with those characters after they've driven the car off the cliff to their deaths? (I suppose you could have an Epilogue that takes place in heaven, with St. Peter saying in a Mel Brooks's voice: "Aaah, what the hell were you thinking?"). But every story will have its "perfect" place for the climax.

And, depending on your plot, the resolution to the whole shebang will fall at the end of the book, with (hopefully) a brief wrap-up. I go with the motto "Quick in, quick out," and that's what I teach my editing clients. The best novels end quickly after the big climax, which is where the protagonist either reached or failed to reach her goal. Since that's the point of the story (to see if the goal is reached), it does a writer no good to wander off into a whole bunch of new plot developments at the end of the book.

I've critiqued novels that have another fifty pages of inconsequential story bits that have nothing to do with the premise of the novel or the protagonist's goal. Bad idea. Readers, after going through the emotional ups and downs of a novel, with the climax bringing everything to a dramatic peak, want that quick and satisfying conclusion so they can let the experience of the journey they've taken with the protagonist sink in and settle.

So, you don't have to break your story up into chunks and have actual sections. But it will help you in the plotting stages to do this in some fashion. Often breaks are best created when there is a jump ahead in time. It could be a week or a year. Again, this depends on your story. Sue Monk Kidd's novel *The Invention of Wings* covers the lifetimes of two women, and so she structured the novel into six parts that each center on a group of significant years, instead of covering every single year in their lives.

Breaks serve many purposes: they allow for a big moment before the end of a section, to set up tension and excitement for the next section that follows, to hint at something coming, to give a breather for the reader to process what just happened (similar to a chapter ending, we tend to pause and prepare to move onward in the story).

Try Laying Out Index Cards to Get a Feel for Sections

Don't just break up a story or create parts to a novel randomly or because someone tells you it's a must. Fashioning your story into sections is extremely helpful, and it's something you can do even if you don't label them as such for your readers.

Sometimes, after I've put all my scene ideas on index cards (as many as I can think of for my novel I'm about to write), I'll lay them all out on my dining table. Usually, as I said, I have between thirty and fifty scene ideas before I start writing my general outline.

Once I have all these cards in front of me, I'll start laying them out in vertical rows. When I get to the place where it feels I've built up to a key plot development that presents "a door of no return" for my protagonist, I'll start a new row with the next scene card.

It's only after I do this that I learn how many "acts" I have.

Does this sound weird? It may, but it works great for me. Maybe it takes experience to know what these big "doors" are and where they should come in a story. And of course, as you get closer to the climax, there are going to be all kinds of complications. So how do you determine where an act "officially" ends?

There are plenty of books and blog posts that can give you insights on this. I find James Scott Bell's *Plot and Structure* a great book to start with, which focuses on the traditional three-act structure. And for the most part I feel it's good for beginning novelists to start there. But just don't get locked into three acts because you've heard you have to.

Here are other examples of sections I created in my novels:

- In *The Map across Time* I use one Hebrew phrase (Hebrew is my forgotten ancient language in my series) and the definition of the phrase as a section break. These five breaks come at the end of a key turning point or development in the story.

- In *Intended for Harm* I have numerous sections, all the names of Bible books and their definitions: Exodus, Numbers, Judges, Song of Songs, etc. I broke up the forty-year family saga into sections, not based on number or years but on milestones the Abrams family faces (death, marriage, tragedy, etc.).

- In *The Hidden Kingdom* I created five section breaks, and in each one they tell a continuing second story line in brief fashion, as the mother (who is one of the characters in the main story line) tells a bedtime story to her son. The bedtime story being told is the novel's story, but it's shared in dialogue and internal thoughts, with the character reflecting on the events that play out in the novel. In other words, I use the section breaks to insert a story within a story.

Note that these are not random choices. They are very specific to the plots of my novels. And each way I handled my section breaks is different. I have section breaks in all seven of my fantasy books in The Gates of Heaven series.

I love the way Orson Scott Card does this very thing but usually with chapter breaks. In *Pathfinder*, my favorite of all his books that I've read so far, he has a whole story unfolding about the spaceship that left Earth to populate a world far away, told in bits at the start of each chapter, while the reader follows the story of what is taking place on that newly colonized world. Both story lines are essential and pull together like threads in a fabric, and in a sense they collide together in a big crash at the end as all the mysteries set up are exposed and made clear.

The key is to let the story define the breaks. Once you have a good overview of your plot, you can use the index cards or some other method to take a step back and see where the natural sections fall.

But . . . all this should lead to determining your ten key scenes. And this is to ensure you have that solid framework. Since it's hard to just sit down and fill out the Ten Key Scene Chart, by doing this bit of brainstorming on sections, it will help prepare you for all the consequent layering you will do.

More Examples of Sectioning

Let's take a look at another of my novels (I'm using mine because I know how and why I created these section breaks.)

In *The Unraveling of Wentwater*, after my prologue (which features a minor character in the past experiencing the Inciting Incident—the baby-naming ceremony that goes awry), we have Part One. In this novel, on the section break pages, I put "excerpts" from the scholar Antius's treatise on The Unraveling of Wentwater. He's a historian and key character in this novel, and these excerpts reflect on the events taking place in the actual story, kind of as an aside.

So Part One kicks off the novel. Part Two comes at about one-third in, at the point where the antagonist of the story sets off to destroy his brother, who has won the heart of the girl he's obsessed with. That first section ends with a huge "door of no return" slamming, for Justyn is now motivated by anger and rejection and is about to set disastrous affairs in motion.

Part Two ends with the huge disaster of the spell gone wrong and the world, essentially, vanishing from existence. Only Teralyn, my heroine, remains, trapped in a magical castle. Another big door, literally, just slammed, locking her in and erasing the outer world. This comes roughly at the two-thirds mark in the novel. And then the book ends with an Afterword, which contains the last bits of wisdom from Antius.

Basically, I used a three-act structure, but I didn't sweat over where exactly these acts fell. I could have added a Part Four section break when Teralyn stitched the world back after seven years and, finally, Wentwater reappeared. But I just kept that whole last section together. In hindsight, I think inserting that Part Four would have made for better structure, giving more impact to the moment when she sees a piece of roofline peeking out of the snowy field. Which shows the flexibility in this method.

Here are the section breaks for *The Wolf of Tebron*, the first book in my fantasy series. All I have on these section break pages are the section titles:

- **Part One: The Lunatic Moon** (comes after the Prologue that sets up the situation in decades past). This covers the setup and the Inciting Incident, which pushes Joran to seek his missing wife and start his adventure, then ends when he arrives at stop #1—the house of the Moon—and then departs.

- **Part Two: The Angry Sun** (about two-fifths in). Joran then travels east to the ends of the world till he gets to the house of the Sun, continuing his search for his wife and collecting new clues.

- **Part Three: The Revealing Wind** (about one-half into the book). Now Joran travels to the cave of the South Wind, where he learns shocking truths about his family and past and loses all hope (leading to his great despair before the push to the climax).

- **Part Four: The Unimaginable Sea** (about four-fifths in) has Joran rescued from captivity, and he's now ready to face his greatest test and fears to snatch his wife from the clutches of the Moon. It's a brief section, which covers the climax and a bit of the resolution.

- **Part Five: The Shortest Way Home** is placed about fifteen pages before the end and is the wrap-up and denouement for the book. It's the final scene.

Joran had five ultimate destinations in his journey. He had to go to the four ends of the world to find his wife, save her, then return home. It seemed logical to organize this novel into these five acts or five sections. I didn't ever consider what page each section would start on or how far into the book they'd be positioned. My "acts" were determined not by the need for commercial breaks but based on the best way I could tell this story.

* * *

Your assignment: Can you break up your novel into sections? How many acts do you end up with? Have you tried putting all your scenes on index cards and laying them out to see what acts seem to appear?

Why don't you give it a try?

If you've already written your novel and you're not sure if you have clear sections or "doors of no return," maybe play around with this. Lay out your scene cards and see if you can develop those key turning points. While we'll be going into the turning points in later chapters, exploring this with a finished novel or in the story development stage is tremendously helpful.

Chapter 3: Premise and the One-Sentence Concept

Before we get into the meat of the first layer of your novel—the ten key scenes—I want to make sure you have a clear understanding of premise and the one-sentence story structure.

We really can't move forward until you have this nailed, so I'll do my best to help you get there.

What's a premise? Simply put, it's a situation that requires a response. Someone with a reason, drive, need, and/or compulsion is required to deal with that situation.

When you generate an idea for a story, you think of an exciting, tense situation that demands that a key character tackle that situation.

You can fashion a premise by asking "What if?" What if a comet was about to hit Earth, and scientists had to find a way to stop it? That idea makes way for a premise (situation setup), which makes way for you to be able to write a one-sentence story concept.

Nail the Point of Your Story

Why should you take the time to put together a one-sentence story concept? Because by distilling your premise into one sentence, you nail the point or objective of your story.

Your one-sentence concept will make it clear what the key situation is in your novel, who will deal with that situation, what's at stake, and what or who is opposing your protagonist.

Remember we looked at the problem and the principal action? That's your one-sentence concept in a nutshell.

How do you go from premise to that important story concept? By adding in those corner pillars of novel construction: the protagonist and his goal and conflict with high stakes.

Many novels I critique each year lack those fundamental story elements. When I ask authors of such a novel to put together a one-sentence story concept, they usually can't. They'll often give a vague explanation of their story, such as "John used to be in the Army but doesn't want to fight anymore, but because of his beliefs, he has to make a hard choice deciding whether to fight evil or spend time dealing with his wife's terminal illness."

While that example seems to have a premise at the center of the story—the goal of fighting evil—it's not nailing the concept. What it hints at is a possibly unfocused premise. And the most important element of a premise is the protagonist's goal.

You Gotta Have Goal

If you don't have a protagonist set up to go after some goal for the novel—a goal that veers the protagonist in a new direction by that Inciting Incident—you are going to have a hard time putting a solid novel together.

Yes, that sounds simplistic. It is. But I will stand by my belief that every great novel is about someone with passion going after a goal. And the premise that's set up (the situation that needs remedying) is all about, yes, that character trying to reach his goal.

There are only five basic story goals for every good story, whether a movie, novel, or play. So at that general place in your story, your hero is now going to try to *get something, stop something or someone, escape from somewhere, win something,* or *deliver something.* I bet you can think of famous movie titles that encapsulate the goal. How about *Escape from Alcatraz* and *Finding Nemo*? Not hard figuring out what kind of goal those stories involve.

If you can't tell me which of those five things your character is after in your story, you may need to stop and do some revisiting of your concept.

Seriously, if even *half* the manuscripts I edited and critiqued had a clear, strong premise featuring a protagonist going passionately after a goal, I would not write so much about this in my blog Live Write

Thrive and my writing craft books. In fact, I'd jump up and down and sing silly little songs if even half of those manuscripts had this very basic and necessary foundation.

So, if you don't have this understanding nailed, spend some time studying up on it until you do. You need to be able to write a one-sentence story concept (yes, one sentence) that tells the premise of your novel, featuring that protagonist and his goal and what conflict or primary opposition he's facing.

Look at this example from *Harry Potter and the Sorcerer's Stone* (via Randy Ingermanson): "A boy wizard begins training and must battle for his life with the Dark Lord who murdered his parents."

Simple and concise. It identifies the protagonist, the premise or situation that must be dealt with, and the opposition in the character's way to reaching his goal.

Some call this a one-sentence pitch a logline (usually for scripts). Scriptlogist.com makes this suggestion:

Here are three questions to ask yourself as you write your logline:

1. Who is the main character, and what does he or she want?

2. Who (villain) or what is standing in the way of the main character?

3. What makes this story unique?

I like Nathan Bransford's simplified formula for a one-sentence pitch: "When [opening conflict] happens to [character(s)], they must [overcome conflict] to [complete their quest]."

Really, is this so hard?

What to Do with All Those Scenes

The most challenging aspect of novel writing, to me, is what to do with all those cool scene ideas and developments. When brainstorming my novels, I often have pages of notes and index cards. I have a ton of great scene ideas that have conflict and show progress and hindrance as the hero or heroine of my story strives to reach the goal.

But then comes the part when I have to lay it all out in the best and strongest fashion.

I don't want to throw all the big rocks, pebbles, sand, and water into the jar in a haphazard manner.

While I now do a lot of this intuitively after having written twenty-plus novels, I still need to break down the action into sections in a manageable way.

And this brings me to the basic framework we're going to start looking at next—the five key turning points in your novel (based on Michael Hauge's story structure).

Along with your Inciting Incident (turning point #1), we'll take a look at the four other key developments in your story, which will help you begin understanding which ten key scenes you need to plan out to begin the framework of your story. Picture those as five big rocks you put into your empty jar.

So, first and foremost: get your premise clear and strong. Practice writing out your one-sentence story concept. If you can't for the life of you figure out what your protagonist is after or what the central conflict is, you more than likely don't have a strong concept, or maybe even a premise. And that's a *big* problem.

If you're stuck and need help, hire me. Let's work on this. You may have a very cool idea, but ideas are lumps of clay. They're just sitting on the table like blobs of potential until you turn them into powerful concepts.

* * *

Your assignment: Write out your one sentence story concept. Work hard on this. Make sure the sentence showcases your protagonist and her goal, the Inciting Incident, the opposition and stakes, and her motivation. Yes, you can get this all into one sentence. Or come up with a logline using the three questions:

1. Who is the main character, and what does he or she want?

2. Who (villain) or what is standing in the way of the main character?

3. What makes this story unique?

Share your sentence or logline with friends, family, and/or other authors and request some feedback. If they don't "get" what your story is about or it doesn't sound all that interesting to them, you may have some work to do on your premise and idea to turn it into a killer concept.

Chapter 4: The First Key Turning Point

So now that you understand what a premise is and what's included in your one-sentence story concept, we next need to take a look at the five key turning points, which are wonderfully explained by story master Michael Hague.

Before we can craft the first ten scenes, we need to understand what these turning points are and where they "fall" in a novel. Some writing instructors insist on exact placement of those points, but as I've said, I believe in flexibility and in letting the needs of the story influence where sections or acts or plot points should go.

Still, by utilizing this structure, however loosely, you can be sure you will have a strong framework for your story, and that's the objective here.

Don't Start Your Novel in the Wrong Place

Writers often start their novel in the wrong place. Many first novels I critique don't have this first turning point at all. Often characters are just going about their ordinary lives without any key event occurring to set up the goal for the novel. Those novels—no surprise—often don't feature a goal of any kind.

This is often the case with fantasy novels in which a character undergoes a journey, and things happen to him along the way. What readers are getting is essentially a string of random scenes showing the ups and downs of a character's life. In other words, there is no point to the story.

Readers expect a point. They expect some Inciting Incident, too, to get the story rolling.

These turning points aren't arbitrary; they're the key milestones of a strong story.

So take the time to understand each of these turning points, which is necessary in order to create your first layer of ten key scenes.

Point 1: "Opportunity"

Let's look at the first key turning point: "Opportunity." Yes, this is the Inciting Incident. Hauge puts it so nicely: "An event occurs that creates desire in the protagonist. Reader gets a glimpse of their longing or need."

Ah, core need. How often I harp on this. Protagonists (and all main characters) need motivation.

We do things for a reason (however wise or stupid), and your protagonist needs a strong reason to chase after her goal. We bond with characters whose needs are clear. We see what they care about, what they're passionate about, what they love to do, what they believe in. But underneath all that is the *need*. A basic, maybe even primal, need.

Every great story has this. Scarlett O'Hara in *Gone with the Wind* needs love. She sure hasn't a clue what it is or how to get it. But it's her core need.

Katniss Everdeen in *The Hunger* Games needs to protect and care for her family. Her core need means she has to be courageous and self-sacrificing.

Atticus Finch in *To Kill a Mockingbird* needs to champion human rights and cannot allow society to pressure him to compromise his core values.

What's your protagonist's need? If he doesn't have one, you're in trouble.

That Inciting Incident, which is designed specifically to shift your character in a specific new direction (to ultimately deal with the premised situation), can't create a "desire" in your protagonist if you haven't fashioned a character who has a strong core need.

In the book *The Martian*, the Inciting Incident has already occurred (though in the film, it's shown in the opening scenes). The protagonist

Mark Watney has been stranded on Mars. What "desire" does that event create in Watney? The desire to survive. That first turning point, that incident, now shifts Watney's former goal (to study Mars and collect samples, then return home with the crew) to a new goal.

Did you catch that? His *former* goal has now been replaced with a *new* goal.

While it's not always best to set up the goal for your protagonist in the opening scene (that's going to depend on your story), you do want that new direction so that by the 25% mark, the goal is fixed.

The Inciting Incident Launches Your Story

Most writers know they need an Inciting Incident or initial disturbance near the start of the book. Yet, I see way too many novels in which there really isn't a strong impacting incident. Or it's in the wrong place.

I recently did a fifty-page critique on a novel (and it wasn't the author's first novel either) that had fifty pages of setup. Backstory. Telling all about how the characters met, fell in love, got married, etc.

What was the stated premise? Basically, it told of a man who has something precious taken from him and must face danger and horror to get that thing back. Huh? What did the first fifty pages have to do with any of that? Nothing.

That Inciting Incident wasn't there. I imagine it shows up at some point later, but that's way too late. The Inciting Incident has to come at the *start* of the story. It launches the story. Catapults it. You don't want your story sitting in that little catapult bucket for weeks just waiting for someone to hit the lever and send it flying.

A ship's voyage begins when it's launched. Not when it's sitting dry-docked for weeks.

Every great story is about some character in his ordinary world that gets veered off in a new or specific direction due to some incident. Life is moving along, and suddenly an opportunity presents itself, for good or ill—or both.

Whether it's a parent's kid getting kidnapped, a violent storm blowing into town, a ship of mutant dinosaurs or zombies that land on shore, or a young woman meeting a hot man, novels need that Inciting Incident to launch the premise.

This really isn't all that hard, right?

Where Does the First Turning Point Occur?

The Inciting Incident or opportunity needs to come at the beginning of your story—before or at about the ten percent mark. If you have a four-hundred page novel (well, you may not yet know how many pages your book will end up having, at this point), that incident is going to show up around page forty. Or sooner.

You don't need to take all that much time for setup, even in a fantasy novel. You just need enough to introduce the protagonist and her world, her core need, the stakes and conflict for the story (personal and public), and the other principal players in the story.

The Hunger Games is a great example. We have the opening scenes showing Katniss with her family, showing the world situation, showing her skill at hunting, showing the two key male characters that will be her love interests. And, boom! The reaping takes place, her sister is chosen for the deadly games, and Katniss volunteers as Tribute in Prim's place.

The Inciting Incident can be big or subtle. It may be one specific scene; it may take place over a few scenes. It all depends on your story. This should answer this oft-asked question: Where should I start my story?

Why, at or directly before the Inciting Incident. Simple.

What Your Setup Isn't

A lot of beginning writers spend chapters setting up their world and characters, explaining the backstory, and boring their readers. Your job as an expert storyteller requires you to know your world and characters and all their backstory but *to hold back almost all of it*. And especially in the opening chapters.

What do I mean here? Most of the info you create on your world and characters should *inform* the story. It should seep through your characters' attitudes, dialogue, behavior, and thought processes. Not told about. Readers want to watch and learn about your characters as they act, respond, process, and opine on what goes on around them.

Too many beginning writers are missing the boat on this very simple structural rule. Just start the story in action, showing something "already happening" in your protagonist's life in a way that reveals him and his situation. Objective: to get your reader to know him ASAP and to be interested in what happens to him.

What the Setup Is All About

The setup is tricky but essential to nail. You have to be concise, succinct, and deliberate regarding what you show and tell about your character. Because . . . you don't want to take a whole lot of time (numerous chapters) to do this. Little bits, small tells, that quickly get your reader on board with your protagonist.

Really, coming up with a starting point for your novel shouldn't be all that hard. Opening scene: set up your protagonist, then hit him with the Inciting Incident. (Now, you may have an opening scene, such as a prologue, that doesn't feature your protagonist, so I'm talking about the first scene with your protagonist, which, if it isn't the first scene, would most likely be the second scene.)

Let's take a look at *The Fault in Our Stars*, a YA contemporary novel by John Green about two teens with cancer who fall in love. A challenging story because, well, it's a depressing topic. So while, one assumes, it would be easy to write a novel that quickly gets the reader to *pity* the heroine, Hazel, the last thing an author wants for his characters is pity.

The Inciting Incident, since this is a romance, is "the meet." Hence, the opening scene shows how Hazel meets Gus.

That first setup scene has to get readers to like and care about Hazel, and Green, a master wordsmith and fabulous writer, gets across Hazel's character powerfully and quickly.

Think about it. Here's a sixteen-year-old girl who basically has a death sentence and has been around dying kids for a few years. She doesn't get to have a normal life. She doesn't get to think happily about her future because she probably won't live into adulthood. To survive, she has to cop a certain hard attitude, yet, for readers to like her, she has to have a measure of self-deprecation balanced with yearning, angst, and misery.

I'm going to share the opening page or two so you can see what a great job Green did in inspiring empathy in readers as well as setting up Hazel's health, character's voice, relationship with family, attitude about life, and the situation she is in that becomes the Inciting Incident.

NOTE: *I'm putting in bold all the important elements that are being set up and that come into play strongly in the plot or serve as repetitive motifs (the latter are important to introduce in the opening scene).*

Chapter One

Late in the winter of my seventeenth year, my mother decided I was depressed, presumably because I rarely left the house, spent quite a lot of time in bed, **read the same book over and over**, ate infrequently, and devoted quite a bit of my abundant free time to thinking about death.

Whenever you read a cancer booklet or website or whatever, they always list depression among the side effects of cancer. But, in fact, depression is not a side effect of cancer. Depression **is a side effect of dying.** (Cancer is also a side effect of dying. Almost everything is, really.) But my mom believed I required treatment, so she took me to see my Regular Doctor Jim, who agreed that I was veritably swimming in a paralyzing and totally clinical depression, and that therefore my meds should be adjusted and also I should attend a weekly **Support Group.**

This Support Group featured a rotating cast of characters in various states of tumor-driven unwellness. Why did the cast rotate? **A side effect of dying.**

The Support Group, of course, was depressing as hell. It met every Wednesday in the basement of a stone-walled Episcopal church shaped like a cross. We all sat in a circle right in the middle of the cross, where the two boards would have met, where **the heart of Jesus** would have been.

I noticed this because Patrick, the Support Group Leader and only person over eighteen in the room, talked about the heart of Jesus every freaking meeting, all about how we, as young cancer survivors, were sitting right in Christ's very sacred heart and whatever.

So here's how it went in God's heart: The six or seven or ten of us walked/wheeled in, grazed at a decrepit selection of cookies and lemonade, sat down in the Circle of Trust, and listened to Patrick recount for the thousandth time his depressingly miserable life story— how he had cancer in his balls and they thought he was going to die but he didn't die and now here he is, a full-grown adult in a church basement in the 137th nicest city in America, divorced, addicted to video games, mostly friendless, eking out a meager living by exploiting his cancertastic past, slowly working his way toward a master's degree that will not improve his career prospects, waiting, as we all do, for the sword of Damocles to give him the relief that he escaped lo those many years ago when cancer took both of his nuts but spared what only the most generous soul would call his life.

AND YOU TOO MIGHT BE SO LUCKY!

Then we introduced ourselves: Name. Age. Diagnosis. And how we're doing today. I'm Hazel, I'd say when they'd get to me. Sixteen. Thyroid originally but with an impressive and long-settled satellite colony in my lungs. And I'm doing okay.

Once we got around the circle, Patrick always asked if anyone wanted to share. And then began the circle jerk of support: everyone talking about fighting and battling and winning and shrinking and scanning. To be fair to Patrick, he let us talk about dying, too. But most of them weren't dying. Most would live into adulthood, as Patrick had.

(Which meant there was quite a lot of competitiveness about it, with everybody wanting to beat not only cancer itself but also the other people in the room. Like, I realize that this is irrational, but when they tell you that you have, say, a 20 percent chance of living five years, the math kicks in and you figure that's one in five . . . so you look around and think, as any healthy person would: I gotta outlast four of these bastards.)

The only redeeming facet of Support Group was this kid named **Isaac**, a long-faced, skinny guy with straight blond hair swept over one eye.

And his eyes were the problem. He had some fantastically improbable eye cancer. One eye had been cut out when he was a kid, and now he wore the kind of thick glasses that made his eyes (both the real one and the glass one) preternaturally huge, like his whole head was basically just this fake eye and this real eye staring at you. From what I could gather on the rare occasions when Isaac shared with the group, a recurrence had placed his remaining eye in mortal peril.

Isaac and I communicated almost exclusively through sighs. Each time someone discussed anticancer diets or snorting ground-up shark fin or whatever, he'd glance over at me and sigh ever so slightly. I'd shake my head microscopically and exhale in response.

So Support Group blew, and after a few weeks, I grew to be rather kicking-and-screaming about the whole affair. In fact, on the Wednesday I made the acquaintance of **Augustus Waters,** I tried my level best to get out of Support Group while sitting on the couch with my mom in the third leg of a twelve-hour marathon of the previous season's America's Next Top Model, which admittedly I had already seen, but still.

Me: "I refuse to attend Support Group."

Mom: "One of the symptoms of depression is disinterest in activities."

Me: "Please just let me watch America's Next Top Model. It's an activity."

Mom: "Television is a passivity."

Me: "Ugh, Mom, please."

Mom: "Hazel, you're a teenager. You're not a little kid anymore. You need to make friends, get out of the house, and live your life."

Me: "If you want me to be a teenager, don't send me to Support Group. Buy me a fake ID so I can go to clubs, drink vodka, and take pot."

Mom: "You don't take pot, for starters."

Me: "See, that's the kind of thing I'd know if you got me a fake ID."

Mom: "You're going to Support Group."

Me: "UGGGGGGGGGGGGGG."

Mom: "Hazel, you deserve a life."

That shut me up, although I failed to see how attendance at Support Group met the definition of life. Still, I agreed to go—after negotiating the right to record the 1.5 episodes of ANTM I'd be missing.

I went to Support Group for the same reason that I'd once allowed nurses with a mere eighteen months of graduate education to poison me with exotically named chemicals: **I wanted to make my parents happy**. There is only one thing in this world shittier than biting it from cancer when you're sixteen, and that's having a kid who bites it from cancer.

I hope you were as "wowed" by this opening as I was. Do we like Hazel? Of course. Yes, we feel pity for her. But we feel more.

She is tough, snarky, but also so sensitive. Doesn't it just break your heart to read that line about her wanting to make her parents happy? She often thinks (and the scenes show) about how much her parents are in anguish over her cancer and impending death. She hates that she is putting them through this, through no fault of her own (yes, it is the fault of the stars—sorry, Shakespeare, you're wrong here).

Her sense of humor is tainted with heavy cynicism, and rightly so. But we don't blame her for that. In fact, we applaud her use of it to stay brave.

The meet? She's already talking about when she met Augustus (Gus), the love interest, close to page 1, but then we get to watch her play out the scene in which she meets him, shortly after this intro. The purpose of chapter one is to reveal the meet—true to solid romance structure (which we'll get to in a later chapter).

But it's also, as I said, meant to hook you into the story via Hazel's character.

All this to say: you need to start your novel where it needs to start, and that's right at or shortly before the Inciting Incident.

Don't have an Inciting Incident? Then you have a BIG problem.

Sure, as a caveat I will say that I imagine there are some terrific novels floating around out there without Inciting Incidents. But honestly, I can't think of any. Can you?

So, that's our first of five key turning points. What is the first turning point in your story? Can you clearly identify it? Does it come near the start of your novel? If not, you have some work to do.

* * *

Your assignment: Identify your Inciting Incident. Write a paragraph or two about this incident and what it needs to accomplish, why it's *the* incident that sets up your premise and launches your story. Answer this: How does my Inciting Incident shift my protagonist's direction? How does it set up the goal to come?

If you don't have an Inciting Incident yet, or yours seems to suck, brainstorm a number of possible scenes/situations for your character that might possibly work. Think: How will you set up your character in that opening scene to reveal her situation and core need and immediate problems/goal such that she will be quickly understood and empathized with? Don't rush this—it's probably one of the most, if not *the most*, important scenes in your novel.

Chapter 5: Turning Points #2–5

Now that you have your first turning point well in hand, you need to consider the second turning point, which occurs at about the 25% mark in your novel. What happens at that key moment? Something that pushes that new desire created at the Inciting Incident in the direction of a specific goal.

Thelma and Louise, in the Inciting Incident (in the movie of that name), feel the need to leave town and go on an adventure, get away from their boring or oppressive life situations. At turning point #2, they leave town.

In many stories, this turning point shows a character leaving one place to head to another. The hero may be setting off on an adventure (*The Hobbit*), the heroine could be starting a new job working for an awful boss (*The Devil Wears Prada*), the hero could be moving to a new town (to deal with any number of things: care for an aging parent, investigate a murder, dig up dinosaur bones). You get the idea.

But your character doesn't have to *physically* move to another location at this turning point. The "new direction" she could be heading in could be taking on a new court case or acquiring a new client. It could be when a mother, having learned (Inciting Incident) that her child has a serious disease, quits her lucrative career to stay at home. But this new direction is created by the Inciting Incident.

In the movie *Baby Boom*, a high-powered New York businesswoman inherits a baby due to a death in the family (Inciting

Incident), and she does all she can to get rid of it. But when it's clear she has to step up and be mom, the goal is fixed for the rest of the movie. She now has to find a way to make her career work with this unexpected shift in her lifestyle.

In *Tootsie*, Michael Dorsey is struggling to make it as an actor (the setup). Desperate, he tries out for a female part in a popular soap opera disguised as a woman. When he gets the part and decides to take it, his goal is fixed. How will he be able to pull it off?

In *The Martian*, stranded astronaut Mark Watney is determined not to die on Mars, while back on Earth, NASA directs satellites to Mars to check to see if there is any sign of life, only to discover Watney is surely alive. In this case, both Watney (protagonist) and NASA (ally) fix their goals at this mark.

From the second turning point up to the Midpoint (50% mark), the character is off on a course to reach her goal. It's about progress and setbacks. It's about encountering opposition.

So now we've looked at:

Turning point #1 - 10% mark (roughly): Inciting Incident

Turning point #2 – 25% mark (roughly): visible goal established for the novel

Turning Points 3, 4, and 5

Turning Point # 3 takes place at the 50% mark or Midpoint. Yes, it's called the Midpoint. The Midpoint is the full "door of no return," which we'll look at closer later. The character is committed; he's all-in. He's gotten a peek of what he's facing in the way of opposition. It doesn't mean he won't slip back, fail, briefly change his mind, or have regrets. A good story will have all that. But it is a pivotal moment of commitment for the character.

Turning Point #4 comes at around the 75% mark. This is the dark moment before the climax. The last push amid the biggest obstacles and challenges. It's the point when the character wants to quit, feels a failure, loses all support, loses his faith, slides back into whatever previous persona gave him false shelter all these years. In other words, things look hopeless or impossible.

This fourth turning point ushers in the final push for the story in which the character has to buck up, rebound from retreat or setback or loss or failure, and draw on every resource and ounce of determination to stay the course.

Of course, every novel is going to vary in degrees regarding this turning point. But the stronger this "dark night of the soul" moment, the more powerful the story.

Turning point #5 is another obvious one, but, surprisingly, a whole lot of novels fall way short here. And that's the big climax. This is the moment when the protagonist either reaches or fails to reach his goal. This is the point in the story when all the internal and external conflict crash head-on and the answers to the two MDQs are revealed.

What's an MDQ, you ask? It's the Major Dramatic Query (or question) you set up at the start of your story (which I explain at length in *Writing the Heart of Your Story*). With every story, you need to have both a visible (plot) query and a spiritual or emotional (inner motivation) query that directly relate to your premise.

If you've structured your novel correctly, you've presented the two questions for the hero: one that speaks to the visible goal and one to the spiritual goal. "Will Katniss win the Hunger Games competition?" (visible goal) and "Will Katniss emotionally survive intact and not compromise her integrity by the end?" (spiritual goal).

Your story may have additional questions that are answered in the climax, such as "Will the hero get the girl?" (a must in romance genres). But all the major questions posed at the start of your story get answered at turning point #5.

Let's take a brief look again at all five points. Keep in mind these percentage marks are not set in stone but are guidelines for basic placement. Your story may require tweaking depending on your plot and genre. You can use this little chart for your assignment below.

Turning Points:

#1: The Inciting Incident or "Opportunity" (10% mark)

#2: The Fixed Goal (25% mark)

#3: The Midpoint (50% mark)

#4: The "Dark Moment" (70-75% mark, right before the climax)

#5: The Climax (75-99% mark)

We'll take a deeper look at these turning points in the next chapters.

* * *

Your assignment: Write down all five major turning points in your novel. Expound for a paragraph or two about each turning point, explaining why they are key milestones in your story. Keep in mind where each turning point is to take place.

Then come up with your MDQs: create two questions, one for the plot goal and the other for the spiritual goal, that must be answered by yes or no at the climax. These will help you home in on your character's motivation and goal for your novel.

Chapter 6: The Power of the Midpoint

Let's examine the next easiest benchmark moment in a novel—the Midpoint. I bet you can guess where this key plot development is supposed to occur in your story.

The Midpoint is often said to take place halfway through the second act. But since we're not breaking things up into three acts here, let's just say it happens right about the middle of your novel. That seems a whole lot simpler to me.

So what's the Midpoint's objective? Basically it's the moment in which something new occurs. Some major development or complication. Some twist or disruption.

Sometimes it's the spiritual or emotional place the protagonist comes to after a series of difficult setbacks or obstacles, where he's pushed to make a hard decision, go through another "door of no return," solidify his resolve, and move into further action. It's a turning point that usually ramps the story up into a higher gear.

Midpoints can also be reversals. Something unexpected happens and changes the worldview of the protagonist. His plan no longer works, and things have to change.

A good Midpoint reversal will also raise the stakes, even if they were already high. It often elevates the personal stakes in a way that wasn't there before or reveals a secret. Sometimes it requires a sacrifice, of a personal belief or an ally. It may involve all these things.

If you've developed a great premise (that concept with a kicker I so strongly preach about), and you brainstorm to come up with a killer Midpoint situation, that can anchor down your framework.

If you have your basics: your Inciting Incident, your protagonist's goal for the book, what is going to happen in the climax and end of the story (how the goal is reached or not, and what those consequences will be), then focusing on your Midpoint can be a great way to zoom in on the heart of your story and character.

Try writing down these basic benchmarks (use my 12 Pillars workbook for an easy, helpful way to do this!) and play around with both the plot and emotional Midpoint elements your story can best use. Think of some big shift for the Midpoint. Something that upends the cart.

Examples of Great Midpoints

The movie *Casablanca* has a terrific Midpoint. Up until that moment, Rick, the bitter, negative, selfish bar owner, has been closed off to everyone and everything else, a bystander watching the war take its toll. At the exact Midpoint of the film, Ilsa comes to Rick's bar after closing. Rick is drunk and treats Ilsa with contempt, reminding her how she'd abandoned him in Paris. Ilsa tries to explain, pleads with him to understand, but Rick will have none of it. She leaves in tears—but only after she shatters his assumptions. Ilsa had left him in Paris because she'd learned her husband, Victor, was alive.

Rick, full of self-disgust, puts his head in his hands, finally facing his demons. "What have I become?" This is the moment of decision. Will he stay a selfish drunk or step up and stand up for something more important than his own little problems (which he later calls a hill of beans)? Everything that transpires in the movie is now impacted by his shift in attitude that occurs at the Midpoint.

In the Midpoint of the lengthy *Gone with the Wind*, we find Scarlett in that "mirror moment," reflecting on how the war has destroyed every vestige of her life, her world, and her home, yet, she still has Tara, her family homestead, and in that moment she determines she will do whatever it takes to preserve and rebuild Tara. This Midpoint, as do many, reveals an internal, personal shift in attitude. Most of the Midpoints in my novels are exactly that.

In the movie *Ghost,* dead Sam learns that his best friend Carl hired the murderer—a shocking revelation that changes and ramps up the conflict. Now that Sam knows who is behind his murder and that his wife is under attack, he is now shifts from reactive mode to assertive attack mode to protect her.

In *Ender's Game*, Ender's apprenticeship in Salamander Army ends abruptly when he is given command of his own Battle School army. This dramatic change in the character's circumstances would have been enough, by itself, to create a solid Midpoint. But Orson Scott Card takes it one step further and complicates Ender's plight by giving him a group of the worst students in Battle School. Dragon Army is designed to test Ender's mettle. The stakes for him are now as high as can be if he is to be victorious.

Mark Watney, in *The Martian*, learns at the Midpoint that the supply probe has blown up. While that dark moment implies all hope is lost, it prompts Watney to now dig in and commit to a higher degree to survive—which will require he come up with a dangerous, impossible plan to traverse Mars for weeks to get to the ARES 4 mission site.

Examples from My Novels

In my earlier novels, I didn't work out my scenes using this layering method or thinking of a specific Midpoint scene. These novels were written a few years ago before I started plotting this new way. So I was pleased to find my Midpoint scenes in the exact middle of my novels.

In my fantasy novel *The Unraveling of Wentwater*, the Midpoint event is when my protagonist Teralyn learns the truth about her past—a shocking truth that upends her world and everything she believes and sends her fleeing. The stakes are raised super high as she runs headlong into danger because of what she's learned:

> As she turned to go, [Antius] laid a hand on her arm. "It may not be wise, Teralyn dear, or safe, to inquire in Wentwater. If the villagers think you are the one foretold to destroy the village—"
>
> Tears splashed hot on his wrist. The storm cloud covering her face burst into a downpour. "All these years, I thought Kileen was my mother And now . . . my real mother is somewhere, who knows where, mourning me, thinking I've been dead . . ."
>
> "Tera—"

Before Antius could dislodge the lump in his throat, she pulled from his grasp and ran down the granite pathway, lost to him before she was even gone from his sight.

In my women's fiction mystery, *Conundrum*, Lisa is searching for clues as to how and why her father died so mysteriously twenty-five years earlier. But her incursion into the past detonates a family conflagration that sets her mother at war with her. Her search for truth exposes deep, dark lies and secrets that threaten to destroy her marriage and her sanity.

The Midpoint finds Lisa learning her mother has taken steps to throw her out of her house and off her precious ranch (which her mother owns). Her husband, Jeremy, in fury storms out of the house. Lisa, reeling in shock, then gets a phone call from local police at the end of the scene, sealing the Midpoint's destruction:

> The voice cut through my speech. "Mrs. Bolton? I need to speak with you about your husband, Jeremy Bolton. Mrs. Bolton?"
> I pulled the receiver away and shook my head as if I had water in my ear. I could hear the officer's voice as I stared at the receiver in my hand. "Mrs. Bolton, are you there? Your husband's been in an accident—"

Up to this scene, Lisa has let things develop between her and her mother without doing much other than reacting. But now she is determined. She will fight her mother with all she has, to save her marriage and her husband. It's war. Game on.

Welcome to the Midpoint.

The Subtle but Powerful Midpoint

Not all Midpoints have to be huge and intense. They can be subtle. The Midpoint in *Despicable Me* shows Gru taking his adopted girls to an amusement park, planning on ditching them. Up till now he's been resisting caring for them. He's evil and heartless, right? He only acquired the girls from the orphanage to use them for his despicable purposes.

But then, cute little Agnes is treated unfairly by an employee at a theme park attraction, and Gru is moved to defend her interests, surprising himself to see how much he's grown to care about the girls and wants them to stay with him after all.

Often the Midpoint is about a tectonic emotional or perspective shift though little is happening in the action itself.

We see this often in romances. In *Ever After*, Danielle finally agrees to an outing with Prince Henry. He takes her to a monastery, where she inspires him with her passion about life. That moment is so understatedly impacting. It is in this moment that Henry sees himself for who he truly is. Danielle quite masterfully mirrors him back to himself, and it both astonishes him and makes him angry. All his years of arrogance and complaining melt into remorse and self-denigration. This moment, which shifts to an attack by gypsies (in which Danielle outfoxes them and saves Henry's life) is the game-changer for Henry, and it influences his decisions for the rest of his life.

In *The Art of Racing in the Rain*, one of my favorite novels of all time, the Midpoint comes at the moment when Denny's cancer-ridden wife, Eve, dies. Keep in mind that Enzo, the dog, is the narrator. He's like the classic chorus we see in Greek tragedies and Shakespeare plays. He observes, he reacts, he gives running commentary.

So, in the novel, Denny is the protagonist; it's his story about how he meets his wife, falls in love, has a daughter, then watches Eve die—which comes at the Midpoint.

Why is the novel set up so perfectly with that event? Shouldn't that be the Inciting Incident?

Good question.

At the 10% mark, Denny has already met Eve and married her. Then, Zoe is born.

Midway through that scene, Eve turns to Enzo and says, "Will you promise to always protect her?" meaning, Zoe, whom she is nursing at the time.

Read what follows. It's interesting:

She wasn't asking me. She was asking Denny, and I was merely Denny's surrogate [Denny is off at a car race when Zoe is born]. Still, I felt the obligation. I understood that, as a dog, I could never be as interactive with humanity as I truly desired. Yet, I realized at that moment, I could be something else. I could provide something of need to the people around me. I could comfort even when Denny was away. I could protect Eve's baby. And while I would always crave more, in a sense, I had found a place to begin.

Why is this interesting? Enzo is acting as Denny's surrogate. This means at the Inciting Incident—Zoe's birth—Enzo, and thus Denny in absentia, is making a promise. The new direction: Denny/Enzo will do everything possible to protect and care for little Zoe.

The Midpoint? Eve dies, so there is no turning back. And this terrible turn of events leads to shock and fear as Eve's parents go all-out in a war to rip Zoe from Denny's arms, even falsely accusing him of crimes in order to get custody of their granddaughter.

A few pages after the exact 50% mark, the next chapter begins with the lines "For Eve, her death was the end of a painful battle. For Denny, it was just the beginning." The beginning of the fight over Zoe.

Instead of seeing Denny's detailed reaction to Eve's death at the Midpoint, we watch Enzo in his grief.

> "She's gone," [Denny] said, and then he sobbed loudly and turned away, crying into the crook of his arm so I couldn't see.
>
> I am not a dog who runs away from things. I had never run away from Denny before that moment, and I have never run away since. But in that moment, I had to run. [Note: Enzo's running is a big motif in this novel, and especially comes into play at the end.]
>
> ... Off to the south, I burst off down the short path through the gap in the split rail and out onto the big field, then I broke west. . . . I needed to go wilding. I was upset, sad, angry—something! I needed to do something! I needed to feel myself, understand myself and this horrible world we are all trapped in, where bugs and tumors and viruses worm their way into our brains . . . I needed to do my part to crush it, stamp out what was attacking me, my way of life. So I ran.

His narrative goes on another page, showing how his grief and rage makes him kill and eat a squirrel (okay, maybe that doesn't sound too "undog-like," but Enzo prides himself on being more like humans). He says, "I had to do it. I missed Eve so much I couldn't be a human anymore and feel the pain that humans feel. I had to be an animal again. . . . My trying to live to human standards had done nothing for Eve; I ate the squirrel for Eve."

Enzo, too, changes at the Midpoint. He, along with Denny, is all-in. And his actions play a key part in helping Denny reach his goal for the novel: to protect and keep Zoe from harm.

Not a typical novel story or structure, with this "dual-character" Midpoint with upped stakes for both, but Enzo and Denny—man and his dog—are in this together for the long haul.

False Peaks and False Collapses

Some people craft their Midpoint with either a *false peak* or *a false collapse* in mind. Whether the Midpoint hints at failure or success, the stakes are now raised.

What's a false peak? It's the appearance of success or victory, only to be quickly upended. Think about the moment in *The Titanic* movie in which Jack and Rose have consummated their love and sworn eternal commitment—only to have the ship hit an iceberg shortly following. The ultimate high and promise of happiness . . . begins to sink into the cold waters of the Atlantic.

In *Gravity*, Ryan Stone, the female astronaut, survives a fire on board the American space station and gets to the Russian capsule (a false peak), only to find that it is also defective. Hopes raised, then dashed, pushing the character to make a hard choice and ramp up her determination to survive.

A false collapse is a huge setback that makes it look like ultimate failure, such is what we see in *The Imitation Game* when Turing's commander orders the computer he's built to be destroyed. But such drastic times call for drastic responses, and the Midpoint is the time to regroup, shift gears, and ramp up the determination.

So be sure when you're crafting your Midpoint that you have your protagonist experience one of two things: a revelation that suggests a far greater obstacle looming on the horizon, or a false peak or a false collapse that propels the narrative toward resolution.

So what about your story? What kind of Midpoint do you have? Is it strong enough? Could it be better? What can you come up with to fashion a killer Midpoint for your story?

Next, we'll look at a few more key moments in your novel structure. This is all leading to those ten essential scenes you'll need to come up with for your first layer.

Take a look at a chart I created to help you lay out those ten key scenes. While we will be going in depth into each one of the scenes, start getting acquainted. You can download the chart as a PDF and/or Excel chart from my resource page at my blog Live Write Thrive.

* * *

Your assignment : Spend some time developing your Midpoint. Play around with both the plot and emotional Midpoint elements your story can best use. Think of some big shift for the Midpoint: a moment in which your character cements his commitment to his goal, ready to give it his all. If your Midpoint is weak, work on making it stronger. You owe it to your story and your readers! Write a summary of your Midpoint scene in your chart.

Chart: First Layer of 10 Key Scenes

#1 - Setup.

#2 - Turning Point #1 (10%) Inciting Incident.

*#3 - Pinch Point #1 (33% roughly).

#4 – Twist #1.

#5 – The Midpoint (50%).

#6 – Pinch Point #2 (62% roughly).

#7 – Twist #2.

#8 – Turning Point #4 (75%) Major Setback.

#9 – Turning Point #5 (76-99%) The Climax.

#10 – The Aftermath (90-99%): The Wrap-Up.

*Note: I don't include a specific scene for the fixing of the goal at around the 25% mark. While the goal should be set about there, it's not necessarily accomplished in one scene. Often it's a series of incidents that "fixes" the goal for the character. But you do want to be sure to layer those important scenes in once you get these ten key scenes set.

Chapter 7: What the Heck Are Pinch Points?

You may have heard of pinch points. Or not. No matter—I'm going to take a look at these key markers because the primary pinch points are two of the ten scenes in the first layer of your novel.

You now understand what the Inciting Incident is and where it needs to come in your novel. And the Midpoint's a fairly easy concept to nail, right? On a map, it would be, well, the Midpoint. The very Middle (the letter M) of the journey from A to Z.

But what the heck are pinch points? Do you need them? Where do they go in a novel, and what's their purpose?

Remember, you want your *story* to dictate how many acts you need and where they start and end. Not the other way around.

That said, there is still the overarching expected novel structure to keep in mind.

Think *road* as opposed to *brush* alongside the road. It's a smoother journey (and more likely you'll make it to your destination less haggard) if you stay on the paved road rather than veer off onto the verge and into the vegetation.

You now understand that your protagonist's goal for the novel should firm up around the 25% mark. But then what?

48

The First Pinch Point

Enter that first pinch point. Somewhere between that 25% mark and the Midpoint, the primary opposition needs to raise its ugly head. Some say it must come at the 37% mark, but you know what I'll say about that.

In engineering, a pinch point is a point between moving and stationary parts of a machine where a person's body part may become caught, leading to injury. That definition applies well to dramatic, literary pinch points. A situation is presented that might have our protagonist "between a rock and a hard place," or, as in this scenario, "between a lever and a cog." Squeezed tight. Potential for (emotional and/or physical) injury. Another definition notes: "There is a chance of entrapment." Nice, right?

Another definition of a pinch point is the place where a road narrows. A driver might be cruising along, when suddenly she is *pinched*—hemmed in on all sides, with no place to pull over. Stopping would be dangerous, and turning around to go back is unthinkable.

The pinch point is all about revealing the force of the opposition. An opposition that eventually, in the story, narrows the means of escape, forces the hero to make hard choices, to take a stand, or to press pedal to the metal and surge to the goal. Or all three.

Whether it's a singular opponent or nemesis; or a natural force, such as a tornado; or an entity or group, such as the legal system or Congress, the pinch point brings to the forefront the opposition.

This helps show how high the stakes are.

Pinch points can also focus on the *emotional change in the character* as he reacts to the new situational development that occurs at these pinch points. Often the protagonist is unaware of what the opposition is doing, but as a result of the events taking place in these pinch points, consequences follow, ones that directly impact him.

Though the first pinch point falls between the quarter mark and the Midpoint, it doesn't necessarily imply you can't show your antagonist earlier in the story, or that this moment is meant to bring full attention on him (or it).

First Pinch Point Examples

Here are some examples of the first pinch point in movies you may be familiar with:

49

- *The Hunger Games*: Katniss enters the game and is attacked, flees, and discovers Peeta has abandoned her and joined a group of killers.

- *The Help*: Miss Hilly announces over coffee that she's going to publish her "Home Help Sanitation Initiative" in the local newspaper.

- *Raiders of the Lost Ark*: Indy thinks Marion is dead. He confronts Balloq and threatens to kill him. Stakes go higher.

- *The Empire Strikes Back*: The emperor tells Darth Vader to hunt down Luke Skywalker.

- *Alien*: The alien detaches from Kane's face and hides in the ship where the crew can't find it.

- *Top Gun*: Right after Maverick screws up big-time on a practice flight, Iceman confronts him in the locker room, pointing out how he's risking lives.

- *The Bourne Identity*: Bourne tracks down the last Treadstone operative, Jarda, who alerts the CIA to Bourne's presence. They fight and Bourne kills Jarda—his first kill in two years—and it shakes Bourne up.

- *Ever After*: Danielle (the Cinderella character) is propositioned by Monsieur LePieu, setting up what is to come at the climax. In addition, Danielle's nasty stepsister Marguerite gets Henry's attention at the tennis match and then almost exposes Danielle as her servant (two pinch points in succession).

- *Taken*: Bryan (father) finds a picture of the Parisian young man who lured his daughter and her best friend into the trap. He attacks the man, demands answers, then chases him down the highway, where the man he must get information from dies in an accident.

- *The Martian*: Mark Watney, alone on Mars, finally communicates with NASA, but his HAB blows up, destroying his food source, making his survival dubious. Mars—not any person—is his nemesis, and Mark is sorely "pinched" when Mars strikes him hard.

The Protagonist's Reaction

This first pinch point is pointing to the main confrontations of your story. It's beginning to show the immensity of the challenge for your protagonist. And often that reveals a big flaw in your protagonist.

Don't miss that.

Think of the pinch point (or the protagonist's reaction to the pinch point) as an opportunity to reveal a potentially fatal flaw in your hero.

Think about that moment in *Top Gun*. Maverick, after being confronted, realizes his serious flaws. If he doesn't deal with them, they could cause disaster. This awareness pushes him to that Midpoint scene.

The result of this new development in your story is centered on the protagonist. Because now he has to do something about this new development, once he learns about it. At this point in your story, he has new information, and that moves him to new action.

In my historical Western *Colorado Dream*, I created a scene in the opposition's POV. My hero inadvertently hurt this rancher's only son, and the young man is now paralyzed. Enraged, Orlander waits for yet another doctor to finish examining his son. When the doctor comes out of the room and confirms there is no hope for recovery, the rancher decides to get revenge by sending his ranch hands after my hero.

Because I used my Ten Key Scene Chart, I knew I not only needed a scene like this (although this rancher has few scenes in the book), and I knew exactly where in my pile of scenes this particular one had to go. Using this layering method takes the guesswork out of the process of plotting a novel. Wouldn't you like to stop guessing?

Don't Forget Action-Reaction

Everything in story—just like the laws of physics—is about action-reaction. Something happens, a character reacts. He decides on a new action because of that, then gets back into action. This is the natural cycle of behavior. We hear or see something, we process, we make a decision, we act.

So as this pinch point reveals something key about the opposition, it—or the results it foments—may cause the protagonist to choose and then act, which barrels the plot toward the Midpoint.

In my Western, my hero has no idea that the "bad guy" is coming after him. It's not until the big blowout gunfight at the fancy party at the climax that he encounters the rancher who is trying to kill him.

But the reader knows. And that's what is most important in my story.

Your story may be different. Your protagonist may experience in person a confrontation with the opposition in that first pinch point.

With a natural event such as a storm or tornado, the stakes are raised and the hero makes a greater commitment to his goal (maybe to save someone in the storm). The point is to show how hard it now is going to be to reach that goal, which should add tension and drama to your story.

Really, all that pinch point is doing is showing the hero progressing toward his goal with the greater stakes and opposition revealed. He might now have more information that can help him defeat his enemy or thwart some complication. Think of the first pinch point as a kind of foreshadowing of trouble to come.

Can you think of a key moment in which you can show your protagonist's central opposition between the time his goal is fixed and the Midpoint scene (which is where his commitment ramps into high gear)?

Don't get all caught up in those specific markers. Just think about the point of your story and that goal your hero is after. It doesn't have to be complicated.

The Second Pinch Point

If the first pinch point reveals the strength of the opposition, the second one showcases the full force of it. If your character faces the edge of a hurricane at sea at the first pinch point, showing him what he's truly up against, the second pinch point is going to be the battle for his life with the full brunt of the storm.

This isn't the climax, but it's building up to it. It's preparing the stage for the final attack, onslaught, or challenge your character will have to take.

Some insist that the second pinch point must come 5/8ths into the story, at the 62% mark, exactly between the middle of the story and the second plot point—the middle of the third act.

Can't we just say this pinch point comes a bit before the climax, to ramp up the stakes and make things start to look impossible for your character? I'm good with that. But, hey, if you need to do the math and put everything on just the right page number, go for it.

Here are a few second pinch points from recent movies:

- *The Bourne Identity*: Bourne returns to the hotel room where he killed Neski and his wife, and there he finally remembers what really happened to him. After the hotel clerk recognizes him, the police break into the room and he barely escapes.

- *The Incredibles*: Helen's plane, which is carrying her stowaway kids, is shot down over Nomanisan Island (I had to read that a few times to get it: no man is an island—ha-ha). Revealed are key facts about the antagonist, Syndrome, and his intent to destroy the OmniDroid and garner glory in the eyes of the Metroville citizens.

- *Ever After*: The wicked stepmother discovers Danielle's deception (pretending to be a countess, essentially lying to the enamored prince) and locks her in the cellar on the night of the ball. A terrific pinch point that cries out "All is lost!"

- *Taken*: Bryan, while searching frantically for his kidnapped daughter, discovers Kim's friend Amanda dead. He tortures the last surviving Albanian and learns Kim has been sold to a French official. Could you think of any better way to show the opposition at full force than this?

Pinch Points Are Key Developments

This basic structure fits every genre. Even a children's fairy tale will show the wolf making inroads in the forest, confronting Little Red on her way to Granny's at the first pinch point. And what happens at that second pinch point? Little Red, having arrived at Granny's house, is noting those big teeth Granny has, followed by the sinking realization that it isn't Granny lying in bed in that cute nightgown and bonnet.

Key plot developments often occur at the second pinch point: a friend dies or betrays the heroine, the key plan to reach the goal falls apart, some unexpected twist throws the biggest obstacle yet in your heroine's path.

Frodo getting chased by the black riders in *The Hobbit* introduces the force of the opposition in the *first* pinch point. But having Gandalf fall into Moria, leaving the fellowship grieved and leaderless, creates an even more difficult situation in the *second* pinch point. New, harder decisions must now be made, and the door to great conflict between the characters has now opened.

The second pinch point in *The Martian* reveals those in opposition to sending the spaceship Hermes on a rescue mission to get Watney. But the flight director goes behind the NASA director's back and secretly informs the crew of the Hermes that Watney is alive and, if they choose, they could attempt a dangerous rescue. They go "rogue" and set a course back to Mars.

In my novel *Colorado Promise*, the second pinch point occurs when my heroine is shocked by the public announcement that she'll be marrying Randall—a coup d'etat by her father, who is her primary opposition in her pursuit of the love of cowboy Lucas Rawlings. Now it seems impossible that Emma and Lucas will ever get together.

As with all my novels, I didn't plan that scene to fall at exactly the 62% mark in my book. I just pulled up my handy desktop calculator, multiplied the total number of pages by .62, and voila!

But, honestly, I don't think in terms of exact pinch point placements. I just think of bigger and bigger conflict to create as my story gallops to the climax. And I make sure I have the opposition coming full-on at these *general* places in the story.

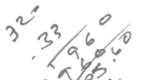

Focus on the Conflict!

So many of these key scenes I'm going to be sharing with you in this layering process are going to center on conflict. And on that action-reaction cycle I mentioned.

Think of those two pinch point moments—one early in your story and one before the climax—in which you can put your character in a vise. Pinch him hard. Make him yell.

When Bruce Wayne's mansion is destroyed and he's left for dead by his nemesis in *Batman Begins*, he's in quite a pinch.

We often see characters in the most hopeless of situations at this point in the story. Play it up, make it big. Make it hurt.

This doesn't have to be a high-action scene though. In a relational drama or women's fiction, this pinch point might look like a heated argument that results in the protagonist losing the support of her best friend, forcing her to make that last push to her goal seem impossible.

* * *

Your assignment: Come up with your first and second pinch points. Think about your key opposition in your story. The first point is where you reveal the power and (possibly) the motivation or intent of this opposition. The second pinch point should bring to the forefront the full threat or power of the opposition (be it storm or evil enemy).

When you're satisfied that you've created the best pinch points write them into your Ten Key Scene Chart.

Chapter 8: Twists and Turns

Twists make good stories terrific. Twists are surprises, reversals. Just when you think . . . then the unexpected comes out of nowhere (or maybe it's expected, but here it comes anyway).

We need to understand how twists work in a story. You'll need two of them—important ones—in the first layer of ten scenes. Sure, you can have more, many more! But you need two impacting twists in your framework.

Call it what you will, but a twist is basically what it sounds like. It's a shift in movement. When you twist your body, you turn in a different direction.

It's a complication. The hero (or any other character) is going along in a direction, and something changes or impedes the forward movement. New information or new developments twist the path being taken.

Plot twists will wrench the current direction of the story in a new, perhaps unexpected direction, and they can vary in strength.

I doubt many writers sit down when plotting and say, "Gee, I need a few twists and turns. Let me list a bunch and figure out where to put them." More than likely they happen as a result of the writer trying to think of interesting *conflict* to add at specific junctures in the story.

If you've been compiling index cards with all your great scene ideas, it's likely some of those scenes are twists.

Where Do Twists Go?

Twists can occur in many places in your novel. The Inciting Incident, in a way, can be considered a twist because it's that first moment that shifts your protagonist in a new direction, presenting a new opportunity. However, it might merely be a situation that prompts the character to get moving—following that action-reaction behavior—rather than an actual twist.

Twists, by nature, are unexpected.

When Charlton Heston's character at the end of the original *Planet of the Apes* movie sees the half-buried Statue of Liberty in the sand, that's a strong twist. It's wholly unexpected, revealing to him and the audience that he is on Earth instead of some strange planet.

When Bruce Willis's character in *The Sixth Sense* realizes he's dead, that's a great twist. It's not just a surprise—because twists are more than that. It's a game changer for the story and what follows in the plot.

Twists, though, don't have to be monumental. In most stories they are going to be small but significant to your characters. They may impact the protagonist primarily, but you can have twists that alter the courses of secondary characters as well.

With thrillers, you may have a dozen small twists and turns that create setbacks for your main character as he pursues his goal. Those twists are the obstacles that keep popping up and forcing the character to steer around, jump over, or plow through to keep making progress.

In this layering system, you are going to have two big scenes with big twists as part of the first ten scenes.

> 80

- **Twist #1** comes somewhere after the first pinch point (at that nebulous or exact 37% mark) and before the Midpoint.

What's Twist #1 about? Something new happens: a new ally shows up, a friend becomes a foe. New info reveals a serious complication in reaching the goal. The protagonist must adjust in response to this setback.

- **Twist 2**, similar to Twist #1, comes after the second pinch point (somewhere around the 67% mark) and before the

> 198

climax. In this twist, an unexpected surprise rears up, giving (false?) hope. The goal now looks within reach. This might be in a mentor giving encouragement, the acquiring of a secret weapon, or the obtaining of an important clue.

A novel may have lots of *small* twists that are basically complications and obstacles the protagonist encounters. But you'll want to have one or two huge twists that wrench the story, and those are terrific when done well.

I've chosen to include two big twists as part of the first layer of novel structure. You may decide you don't want or need those twists. But before you decide, why not try to come up with something and see how it works in your story framework? I think you'll be glad you did.

Misdirect with a Plot Twist

Twists are all about redirection—or misdirection. Going against expectations.

Think about what readers are expecting and hoping for at a given moment in the story. Then keep tweaking the story into new directions that stun and delight them.

If your POV character is seeing indications that her boyfriend is going to propose to her—he's invited her to a special dinner, says he has something important to tell her, etc. —she's going to get her hopes up. The more you, the author, can imply that's the boyfriend's intention, the more impacting the twist will be when he shows up at the restaurant and tells her, sadly, that he has to call it quits. That his long-lost love he thought dead was really alive and well in Chicago ("we'll always have Paris . . .") and he just happened to bump into her at the dry cleaners. Or something like that.

To keep readers from noticing clues, bury them in the emotion or action of another section. For example, in an adventure novel, offhandedly mention something during a chase scene, while readers' attention is on the action, not the revelation. Then bring it full frontal later on.

Think about casting suspicion on other characters. This is good misdirection. Another's actions can be suspect, misinterpreted. Someone running out of a coffee shop can assumedly be meeting a lover clandestinely when he is actually responding to a call that his mother has been rushed to the hospital.

Having characters jump to conclusions, make emotional judgments, fail to see the obvious because of emotional issues—these can all help when creating twists. An insecure character will think her best friend has abandoned her when he doesn't show up, and that can push her to reactions and actions that will send her off in an unexpected direction.

This morning, before working on this book, I continued plotting out my next Western in my Front Range series, *Wyoming Tryst*. This exact situation comes into play when my hero, Robert Morrison, rides into Laramie to meet with his beloved so they can marry. When he can't find her and no one knows where she's gone, he quickly assumes she jilted him.

Why? Because at the start of the novel we see Robert's friends trying to lift his spirits after a woman jilted him. Instead of looking further and discovering that she's been hauled off to prison for shooting a would-be rapist in self-defense, he leaves town and heads to Colorado, hurt and angry. This makes the way for another great plot twist and crisis of conscience when he reads in a newspaper that his Julia, daughter of another prominent ranching family, is slated for execution, incarcerated at the territorial penitentiary.

(I'm doing *Romeo and Juliet* a la Wyoming in the 1870s, so you might recognize this as the early scene in which Romeo is walking the streets of Verona upset over being ignored by Rosaline.)

Make Those Twists Believable

The best twists work because the reader has been led to believe in the certainty of a situation or outcome. By pulling that out from under the reader (and set up believably with those earlier hints), the twist will cause that shock and surprise, but it will work (so long as you don't lie to your readers). And you don't want readers to be angry or upset at a stupid or unbelievable plot twist. If your readers say, "Aw, come on—that character would never do that" or "That just would never happen," then your twist isn't well constructed.

I read a best-selling novel that had a big twist at the end that was so unbelievable, I got angry and threw the book across the room! I had loved *The Horse Whisperer* . . . up until the love interest killed himself in order to spare the heroine from having to choose between him and her husband. I kid you not (Redford changed the ending in the movie, and wisely so!).

In other words, don't use a stupid, unbelievable twist just for shock value. Think through your twists, and make them work to your benefit.

No, they're not all that easy to do, but spend time thinking about creating twists in your story. As with any key development in your novel, you can make a list of five or more expected outcomes of a choice or action. Then study those and think how you could perhaps use the opposite of one.

What could make a close friend turn on your protagonist? Something she misheard? Something she needs or longs for that comes within her grasp that makes her choose that thing over supporting the protagonist? Speaking of *Romeo and Juliet*, could there be any better example of a story rife with misdirection, wrong assumptions, and unexpected twists? I think not. (Don't worry, in my novel, being that it is a sweet romance and not a tragedy, my characters don't end up dead! But it's gonna be close!) Which also prompts me to encourage you to study the great classics—novels and plays.

In the Spanish play *Life Is a Dream*, written by Pedro Calderón de la Barca , a contemporary of Shakespeare's, Segismundo, prince of Poland, has been imprisoned in a tower by his father, King Basilio, following a dire prophecy that the prince would bring disaster to the country and death to the king. Basilio briefly frees Segismundo, but when the prince goes on a rampage, the king imprisons him again, persuading him that it was all a dream.

Similar to *Oedipus Rex*, the prince, in attempting to thwart a prophecy, causes the prophecy to be fulfilled. These are great plot twists that would be featured prominently in the Ten Key Scene Chart, without a doubt.

What If Readers Figure Out the Twists?

Now, some readers may figure out your plot twist early, and that's fine—so long as your plot twist really advances the story and creates intriguing drama. You can have readers for dozens of pages biting their nails because they've figured out (they think) the twist, and now they can't wait to see what happens when the character learns the truth.

I have lots of powerful plot twists in *The Map across Time*, which is probably one of the reasons it's my favorite of all my novels. I took all the major plot elements—the mystery of the queen's "death" (did she really die?), the firebird's strange appearance (what really is the firebird?), the magical map (who made it?), the stranger that instructs Adin (who is he?)—and twisted them all. The entire book is a twist. And by the end, all the twists lay out in a flat line of clear, concise story.

Work on coming up with twists for those two key scenes in your first layer. Then think how to set them up well earlier in the story. Keep in mind, though, that your story and genre might lead you to put that big twist in at the end, even after the climax.

Jodi Picoult's novel *My Sister's Keeper* had two potent plot twists at the end—one pertaining to the actual plot events (the accident) and the other the reveal about Anna's true motivation for wanting to stop being a donor for her sister, Kate, who has leukemia. Picoult's book is the perfect example of setting up readers' expectations and beliefs such that these twists, so cleverly built into the story, hit hard.

The movie *Outbreak* comes to my mind with twist #2. Dustin Hoffman's character finally finds the monkey carrying the disease. He flies to the noted location, and the monkey is caught. They now have great hope to get a cure made before everyone in the quarantined town (and possibly the world) dies.

But . . . he learns upon returning that the president has authorized full cleansing, and the bomb is en route to annihilate the town. Hope is raised but then so are the stakes, and that propels the story toward turning point #4—that major setback or crisis at the climax.

There's nothing more fun than raising someone's hopes to the heights, then dashing them. No, I'm not mental. This is good storytelling!

Raise your character's hopes at a moment when he really needs hope. Then smash it into pieces and send him reeling. That's the build to the climax.

Red Herrings

In lieu of a twist, you might throw some red herrings in to misdirect a character (and reader) and lead him off track. Just as a strong smell of fish might cause a hunting dog to detour from his path of finding a downed bird, a strong misdirection can throw off a character, or your reader.

A red herring is a common device used in mysteries and thrillers to distract the reader from identifying the real culprit. The red herring may be a character that the reader suspects due to misdirection by the author but who turn out be innocent when the real murderer is identified. But red herrings can be used in any novel as a way to complicate the plot and interfere with the protagonist reaching her goal.

In *The Da Vinci Code,* we see the protagonist, Robert Langdon, certain that Bishop Aringorosa is the one killing people to find the Holy Grail. This belief distracts both Robert and the reader from the unexpected mastermind of the plot: Sir Leigh Teabing, the frail old man and mentor of the hero.

In the movie *Legally Blonde,* Elle Woods—erstwhile bimbo, now aspiring attorney studying at Harvard—is helping in a trial defending Brooke Wyndham, who is accused of killing her husband. Brooke can't give an alibi, and her stepdaughter has told an eyewitness account of Brooke standing over the dead body with gun in hand, so it looks pretty bad for Brooke. However, when Elle goes to visit Brooke in prison, Brooke confides that on the day of the murder, she had liposuction—something the famous fitness guru wouldn't dare let the public know. Elle eliminates the red herring, which leads to her solving the murder.

Red herrings can also be objects, such as a piece of clothing, a ring, or a book. But when you're laying out our ten key plot scenes, you want to come up with a red herring—should you choose to use one—that causes a twist in the action, and usually in the protagonist's or in another's that directly impacts his path.

Red herrings are great elements that create twists, but too many of them can muddle a plot and create lack of focus. But one of your key twists in your novel could be a red herring—if it fits your genre.

Unreliable Narrator and Smoking Guns

I love the image that comes to mind with the term "smoking gun." If you see a smoking gun in a person's hand when you walk into a room, it's weighty evidence that the person just fired that gun. "Smoking guns" can be effective in twists because of the misdirection they create.

In my detective novel *A Thin Film of Lies,* Mike Jepson is arguing with his wife in his front yard when the police show up to check the dent on his front car bumper. Tiny threads from the sweater the victim Libby Denham was wearing are carefully collected and submitted as evidence that Mike hit and killed her with his car. But it's a smoking gun. And one that, complied with other "smoking" bits of "evidence," land Mike in jail for manslaughter.

A plot twist could be the result of an unreliable narrator. I found *Gone Girl,* while highly disturbing, impressive due to the twist created by the unreliable (read: flagrant liar and psychopath!) female lead in the story. You are way into the book by the time you learn the cold, scary truth about Amy Dunne.

In *The Girl on the Train,* we see a number of plot twists, red herrings (the doctor who Rachel thinks may have killed Megan, for example), and an unreliable narrator (who turns out to be not so much) due to her excessive drinking habit. A brilliantly structured novel—a murder mystery—that uses those important plot twist scenes in all the right places.

Don't Forget to Properly Set Up Your Twists

While plot twists need to be surprising, they should be properly set up. Meaning, if you are going to have that "smoking gun" show up late in the story, you need to show a hint of it early on. Anton Chekov said, "One must never place a loaded rifle on the stage if it isn't going to go off. It's wrong to make promises you don't mean to keep."

Think about including one or two strong twists in your story, but be sure to set them up.

All the clues are there to show that Dr. Crowe in *The Sixth Sense* is dead—young Cole tells him directly: "I see dead people" as he's looking right at Crowe. I sure missed the obvious there!

The best twists are the ones that cause readers to say, "Oh, I should have seen that coming!" But, of course, you don't want your reader to see it coming. You want that twist to hit her smack on the head. But if you hint enough earlier, the payoff is fantastic.

Which is what makes Turow's breakout novel *Presumed Innocent* so terrific. Turow gives so many great clues to indicate who murdered Carolyn Polhemus—and the murderer is a huge surprise—that when you finally, in the end, learn who that is, you realize it was obvious. Yet, both readers and characters in the story are absolutely blindsided by this revelation. No wonder it topped the best-sellers lists for months.

* * *

Your assignment: Come up with at least three great twists for your novel. Play around with the idea of a red herring or two. Who can come across as an ally but really be an antagonist (or vice versa)? Think of some ways you can drop hints early in the story that misdirect or mislead (without lying to or betraying the reader). Then consider how you might place two of those plot twists in the appropriate places in your layer.

Remember: **Twist #1** comes somewhere after the first pinch point and before the Midpoint. This is where something new happens: a new ally appears, a friend becomes a foe. New info reveals a serious complication to reaching the goal. The protagonist must adjust in response to this setback.

Twist 2 comes after the second pinch point and before the climax. In this twist, an unexpected surprise rears up, giving (false?) hope. The goal now looks within reach. This might be in a mentor giving encouragement, the acquiring of a secret weapon, or the obtaining of an important clue, for example.

When you're happy with what you've come up with, write these twists in your chart.

Chapter 9: The Dark Night, Climax, and Resolution

While the purpose of these last key scenes may be somewhat obvious, there are some aspects we should keep in mind when crafting the "dark night" moment and the climax of our story. These are the big powerful scenes the entire story is barreling toward, and it's important we structure them carefully for greatest impact.

The Dark Moment Showcases Your Themes

I haven't spoken about theme in this book, but it's an essential pillar of novel structure. Even a suspense thriller that appears to be just a hang-on-to-your-seat wild ride of chases and danger can present themes that readers resonate with. Just take a look at the popular superhero movies—they're all about good defeating evil, one of the most ubiquitous themes in stories.

Theme is what your story is "really about." Theme is your protagonist's inner motivation made universal. So it stands to reason that in that key scene #8—the "dark night of the soul" moment—your novel's theme is going to come to the forefront. The dark moment of despair or hopelessness often reflects back the theme by showing exactly how the character feels about the pertinent issues in her situation.

So when you're brainstorming that dark moment and your climax, think about your themes, and have your character face full-on the things that matter most to her and what is ultimately driving her to her goal.

Make It Impossible

In this dark moment, we need to think of all the ways we can make this situation as hopeless as possible. Everything the character has depended on up till now should fail.

Once the character feels all is lost and processes the situation she is in, she essentially looks back on the journey so far—what brought her to this brink of failure—and questions her commitment, beliefs, choices, and actions. If "all is lost" at this crisis point, it only stands to reason she is going to look at how she got here and what possible options there are, if any, for going forward.

Now, at this crucial point in the story, the plan to reach her goal has failed, the obstacles are insurmountable, and the character thinks, "There's absolutely no way out." If you're writing a romance, this is the moment the hero loses all hope of getting the girl. In a mystery, arriving at the truth seems impossible. In a thriller, evil seems to have won.

At this point, too, there's no retreating or going back—the only way out is through. And that means one final hard push toward that goal—often lacking the support of allies the character once had. Often the hero has to go it alone—everyone else is either dead or has abandoned him.

Make It Believable

Readers love it when we paint our heroes into a corner that is seemingly impossible to get out of. And that's the challenge of the dark night moment and climax. But we need the situation and the solutions to be believable. If you are going to have your character use some talent or skill or amazing intellect to prevail, you better make sure you set up throughout the story that he has that needed attribute.

If you're going to have another character suddenly show up and save the day, that's not going to work. Your hero has to be the one to draw from his well of inner resources to push through to victory. Yes, an ally can show up to give support—think of how Hans Solo comes "out of nowhere" in *Star Wars* to help Luke Skywalker in that eleventh hour to destroy the Death Star. But Luke is the hero, and it's his goal we're focused on. He saves the day by trusting the force and firing the explosive that blows up the Death Star.

The Moment of Truth

Part of the dark night moment is the transition from hopelessness to determination. This is the "moment of truth" that comes right before the outward, visible action taken to reach the goal. The decision to press on is made in that "moment of truth." Does she really want to reach that goal? What's it's worth to her? What will it truly cost her? What will the consequences be if she fails? Who will suffer?

With lighter stories, you're not going to have car chases and a high death count as your hero races toward the goal.

At the end of *Never Been Kissed,* Josie is standing on the pitcher's mound with the clock ticking. She has alienated the guy she loves and has exposed her heart by revealing her ruse (pretending to be a high school student) via an article she wrote for her newspaper. Will Sam forgive her and come to the ballpark before the clock counts down to zero? Everyone in the crowd is waiting and watching with her, hoping he'll come. Her heart is on the line, but he's not there . . . then, he runs toward her. Whew!

You still need to wrap up the climax by showing what is going on around the hero once he gets to the goal line. The world may continue crumbling around him, but he finds a way out. The girl might get the guy, but they still have to kiss, let everyone cheer them, then take their bow. The moment needs to be resolved in a satisfying way.

Here are a few movies with great climax moments:

It's a Wonderful Life: George's dark moment brings him to the revelation of seeing what the world would have been like if he wasn't in it, and this then moves him to run back to the bridge where he was going to jump to his death and instead cries, "I want to live again!" From there, the town comes together at the climax to help George raise the lost money so he can avoid arrest.

Ender's Game: After Ender completes his training and practice sessions, the big battle against the Formics takes place. Under the greatest duress, Ender vents his anger and destroys the enemy, thinking he is only trying to pass a test. His dark moment occurs when he learns the truth—that he actually annihilated an entire species and their home world. While the big battle appears to be the climax, it's a "faux" climax. For Ender, his goal is reached and his arc is complete when he rescues the queen pupa and heads off to a planet to ensure the survival of her species.

Master and Commander: The Far Side of the World: The final climactic battle between the *Surprise* and the *Acheron* builds to the moment in which Jack discovers his captain, his long-pursued enemy, is dead. He takes the captain's sword from the surgeon and begins repairs.

It's important to keep in mind that the climax may not be just one scene; it could comprise a number of scenes. But when coming up with your ten key scenes, focus on *the* moment in which the goal is reached. The climax brings the conflict with the opposition to a close. And it's also the moment when the two MDQs are answered, so the protagonist comes into his essence in full in that scenes. This is where he faces the truth about himself and his world.

If your character is victorious at the climax, he will reaffirm his beliefs, embrace his truth, defeat his lie about himself and the wound that has hounded him. He may be hurt and in pain, but the valuable lessons learned outweigh the damage.

Key Scene #10 – The Satisfying Resolution

After climax, your story is over. The hero has reached (or failed to reach) his goal, the conflict has ended, the plot has reached its basic conclusion.

But if you end your novel there, readers will put down your book unsatisfied. That final essential scene is needed for closure and wrapping up the loose ends.

Whether that resolution scene comes moments after the climax or skips ahead months, you want a succinct, brief scene that shows the *results* of the hero reaching his goal and brings your theme(s) to the forefront one last time.

You want to leave readers with a specific feeling or emotion. This is the period at the end of the sentence, the last note that lingers in the air after the end of a sublime symphony.

Ask yourself: Will your story ending leave readers happy, sad, or somewhere in between? Will you tie everything up, or do you plan to leave some things hanging because you're doing a series?

Keep this in mind too: a story that is completely resolved in the final pages can feel too pat and perfect. If everyone at the end is ecstatically happy, that's not always a good thing. Hinting at change to come, at positive prospects, can be much more rewarding—and realistic—than that pat ending.

At the end of *Colorado Hope*, we see my hero and heroine at the park where a big celebration is underway. Colorado has been declared the 38th state, and the lovers are with their friends—those who helped stop the bad guys and reunite the pair. However, Alan, a young man who had a crush on the heroine and who played a key role in getting the lovers back together, shows up with a gal who seems to take a keen interest in him, hinting that Alan, too, will find true love . . . perhaps soon.

I like to think of the resolution scene as the final curtain in which all the key players take a last bow on stage. This of course is going to depend on your genre and plot. But I find it helps to think in this way so I don't leave anyone out. The supporting cast often needs to be acknowledged in the end by the hero—and the reader.

Sometimes additional scenes will show the aftermath of some of the characters, including the villain, if appropriate. But you want to end with your hero enjoying the rewards of having reached his goal. More often than not, it's within that scene that the opposition is shown to be fully defeated or impotent. Picture that deflated bad guy slinking away from the party, muttering angry words and looking wholly pathetic. Or the nemesis being dragged off by the cops to jail as the hero and his crew look on and smile.

While following that adage "Quick in, quick out" is wise, don't rush your climax and resolution scenes. Often writers are burned out and exhausted from all the hard work of writing an entire novel, and they tend to hurry through these last scenes. But they're some of the most important, so take your time to craft them well.

* * *

Your assignment: Work on the key scenes #8-10. Spend time thinking of ways to make that dark moment as hopeless as possible. Think of your themes and how your protagonist can ponder her values and beliefs so that you bring the themes to the forefront. Lay out a powerful, impacting climax scene that shows your character reaching or failing to reach her goal. Then come up with that satisfying resolution scene that shows the aftermath of the climax.

* * *

You're now ready to dig into layering! I hope you've been putting your scenes into the chart and you now have a good understanding of both what types of scenes are needed for this initial framework as well as where they are positioned in your novel.

If you haven't taken the time to develop a strong concept with a kicker, the protagonist and his goal, the conflict with high stakes, and the themes with heart, you should hold off going any further until you do so. Think about studying my *12 Key Pillars of Novel Construction* and use the workbook to flesh this all out. Then you'll be ready to dive into laying out all these scenes.

Here are those ten scenes in a chart with a bit more explanation. (You can download a PDF at www.livewritethrive.com—you'll find the link on my resource page.)

The Ten Key Scene Chart Elaborated

#1 **Setup.** Introduce protagonist in her world. Establish her core need. Set the stage, begin building the world, bring key characters on stage.

#2 **Turning Point #1** (10%) Inciting Incident. This starts the protagonist moving in a new direction. It's the "opportunity" that arises.

 Turning Point #2 (25%) The goal is set.

#3 **Pinch Point #1** (33% roughly). Give a glimpse of the opposition's power, need, and goal as well as the stakes.

#4 **Twist #1.** Something new happens: a new ally appears, a friend becomes a foe. New info reveals a serious complication to reaching the goal. Protagonist must adjust to change with this setback.

#5 **The Midpoint – Turning Point #3** (50%). No turning back. Important event that propels the story forward and solidifies the protagonist's determination to reach her goal.

#6 **Pinch Point #2** (62% roughly). The opposition comes full force. Time to buckle down and fight through it.

#7 **Twist #2.** An unexpected surprise giving (false?) hope. The goal now looks within reach. A mentor gives encouragement, a secret weapon, an important clue.

#8 **Turning Point #4 – Dark Night Moment** (75%). Major setback. All is lost and hopeless. Time for final push.

#9 **Turning Point #5 - Climax** (76-99%). The climax in which the goal is either reached or not; the two MDQs are answered.

#10 **The Aftermath** (90-99%). The wrap-up at the end. Dénouement, resolution, tie it all in a pretty knot.

Part 2: The Next Layers

Chapter 10: The Next Layer

This is where it gets fun and crazy—once you've locked in your ten foundational scenes. Meaning, you have all kinds of options here when it comes to layering your scenes.

In thinking of various genres, I came up with all kinds of possibilities. So I'm going to throw a few at you and let you play with this.

I'll show you an example of using that natural action-reaction behavior to create the second layer. We'll also look at romance structure using this technique (since romance novels have two different engines that drive the story), and I'll show you how I focus on subplot for my second layer in my crime/detective novel.

No, your layers don't have to always comprise ten scenes, but it's an easy and practical method. I happen to like simple methods with round numbers. Feel free to vary this. But I'll be presenting some options here, and I hope they'll help you flesh out your novel in an organized and intuitive way.

Some novels have fifty scenes; some have more than a hundred. But it makes sense to me to start with the most important ones and work your way to the small ones—the ones that link the bigger scenes.

Or, revisiting the analogy I started with, we start filling the jar with big rocks, then drop in pebbles, then sand, then water. Then the jar is full.

I like to layer in subplots, and I'll be providing you with a twenty-scene chart and an example to show you how you might do this with your story. But if your novel doesn't have a subplot—like *The Martian* or *Cast Away*, which are singular plots about a man trying to survive the elements—you'll need a method of layering that is directly related to your main plot. Or you might opt for this layering option over the subplot one, even if you have a strong subplot. The objective is to use a layering method that works best for your story.

You can get very complex with all this, but if you're new to writing novels, I would encourage you to start simple. I've seen too many aspiring novelists attempting extremely complex plots and failing miserably due to a lack of skill and experience in structuring novels.

What I find the easiest and most logical when it comes to this second layer is to think in terms of that natural action-reaction cycle. You can start fleshing out your plot outline by padding the ten key scenes with the reaction and processing scenes.

For example, take a look at the scenes numbered 11-20 (in boldface) that I've interspersed in the first layer chart.

Chart: Action-Reaction Second Layer

#1 Setup. Introduce protagonist in her world.

#2 Turning Point #1 (10%). Inciting Incident.

#11 Reaction to the Inciting Incident. Character processes, makes a decision, leads to . . .

#12 Turning Point #2 (25%) – New action or incident that sets the goal for the novel.

#3 Pinch Point #1 (33% roughly). Give a glimpse of the opposition's power.

#13 Reaction to the Pinch Point or first big step toward the goal. (Note: often the protagonist isn't aware of the action occurring in the pinch point, so instead you might show some initial steps taken toward the goal.)

#4 Twist #1. Something new happens. Protagonist must adjust to this event.

#14 Character acts based on that twist (the adjustment played out).

#15 A complication because of the adjustment.

#5 The Midpoint – Turning Point #3 (50%). Important event that solidifies the protagonist's determination to reach her goal.

#16 Regroup after the Midpoint, a decision made for new action.

#17 A new complication and reaction.

#6 Pinch Point #2 (62% roughly). The opposition comes full force.

#18 Response to the big challenge presented by the pinch point.

#7 Twist 2. An unexpected surprise giving (false?) hope.

#19 Adjustment to the twist. Decision and new action.

#8   Turning Point #4 (75%) Major Setback. All is lost and hopeless.

#20 Help or strength comes to succeed at the climax. Prepare for the final push.

#9   Turning Point #5 (76-99%) The Climax.

#10 The aftermath (90-99%) The Wrap-Up.

I hope you can see the many possibilities here. While these descriptions are a bit vague, they capture the progress and setbacks as the protagonist goes after her goal. Two steps forward, one step backward. Your novel will have a mix of action and inaction. Of doing and of processing or thinking, regrouping. In those low-energy processing scenes, that's where we see reflection and growth. Those pertain to the character arc.

With every new action or twist or setback, your character needs to react, process, and make a new decision. Plans are revised. Internal goals are questioned, character flaws and strengths are revealed and put to the test.

Your character will have momentary victories, but she'll also have failures. I like to build my stories so that each setback or failure is bigger and more impacting than the last.

One prolific author I know plots her novels with three main obstacles, each worse or more challenging than the prior one, with the final one at that dark moment before the climax. That's a great initial framework, but you can certainly have many more than three complications along the way.

Chart Out Those Scenes of Best Sellers

To get a more specific idea of this next layer, think about grabbing a few best sellers in your niche genre—novels that are as similar to your story as possible. Read through these novels and jot down a brief summary of each chapter's plot. When you're done, you should be able to identify those ten key scenes.

I say "should," but, as you'll see in the last part of this book, sometimes even highly touted blockbuster novels can fail miserably when it comes to structure.

Sad, but true—there are a lot of successful novels that have a weak or flawed framework, and often it's a mystery to me why they've succeeded. There could be many reasons for that, which I'll discuss later.

Hopefully, though, you'll find some novels that have all the ten key scenes in place.

As you study these novels, you can also get some great insights into those adjacent scenes that show how the character reacts and then initiates new action due to the main plot events that transpire.

This isn't a waste of time.

Honestly, we writers need to do our homework. If we're going to write in a specific genre, we need to know what the basic plot structure is for that genre.

While there will be room for variation within a genre, you're going to see some very clear similarities. An international thriller is going to have a lot of high-action scenes with very few processing ones. Characters in those types of novel briefly process while they're jumping out of airplanes or planting bombs. In contrast, a thoughtful women's fiction novel is going to have a large number of low-energy processing/reaction scenes that reveal inner conflict.

So take time to figure out where your novel fits into genre, then do your homework. Use these charts to identify their five turning points and their ten key scenes. Make a mark or highlight the secondary scenes that seem the most important. That's where you'll find the second layer.

An Analysis of *Catching Fire*

I spent some hours going through Suzanne Collins's novel *Catching Fire*, the second book in her Hunger Games trilogy. If I were planning to write a dystopic novel (especially a series), this would be a good choice.

After I listed a summary of all the chapters (which have only one scene per chapter, though Collins does do leaps of time in some of them, noting multiple incidents and developments), I took a look at the *placement* of these scenes as well as the type of scene they were. I determined which were the ten key scenes.

Take a look at what I came up with. I hope you can see how this exercise might be insightful and instructive for you, to help you nail your genre's *typical* structure.

Collins was spot-on. I used my handy calculator to determine the page numbers for each of the key scenes, and those scenes are exactly in the right place.

Note: because this is the second book in a trilogy, *Catching Fire*'s plot goal is reached (Katniss yet again survives the deadly games), but the ending has a *big twist*, and readers are denied key scene #10—the resolution or denouement. That "happily ever after" scene can't come until the end of the series, with the overarching goal being the takedown of the Capitol and a "brave new world" of hope being reached.

Catching Fire
By Suzanne Collins
Book 2 in The Hunger Games series

1. **Key Scene #1 – Setup.** Katniss reflects on the changes to her life since arriving back from the Hunger Games. She brings food to Gale's family and spreads her wealth around. She reinforces her relationship with Haymitch, waking him from his liquor-induced slumber. Peta arrives with bread. Katniss's uncertainty regarding her feelings for Peta is evident.

2. President Snow shows up at Katniss's house. He indicates he would have preferred her (and Peta's) death at the end of the Hunger Games as he grills Katniss. The conflict/stakes are established as high as ever.

3. Katniss PROCESSES what just happened. She attempts to make sense out of her exchange with President Snow while she bathes in preparation for her prep team's arrival. The trio arrives to prepare Katniss for her tour of the districts. Katniss is encouraged to develop a talent. Peta and Katniss exchange a kiss before the cameras. Haymitch tells her she will never have a real life—the one she wants with Gale.

4. **Key Scene #2 - Inciting Incident.** On the train, Katniss details the recent visit with President Snow to her team. She runs through her next moves and options. At District 11, they do their act. Peeta surprisingly offers the district a portion of their winnings. Then Katniss speaks consolingly to the crowd, which responds by showing solidarity with the mockingjay salute. **Katniss realizes she's unleashed the whirlwind and in horror watches a man shot because of her.**

5. They hurry back into the Justice building as more shots are fired. Haymitch demands to know what happened. Peeta explodes in guilt. Quick montage as they spend days doing the same

appearances at all the other districts, until they arrive at the Capitol, where they make their final appearance before Snow.

6. They attend the big party at Snow's mansion. Katniss thinks about the suffering people. Scene ends with her seeing a secret transmission showing a violent uprising in District 8.

7. Katniss remembers when she was in the woods on her way to the cabin for a rendezvous with Gale. Gale and Katniss draw closer, and Gale announces his love for her. Katniss tells Gale about the uprising in District 8. Gale reacts strongly. Katniss tells of her plan to run away. They argue about options, the world predicament. Coming out of the woods, Katniss seeks out Peeta to explain her plan and seek his approval. Gale is whipped in the square for his transgression of hunting in the forest. **[This is also the 25% mark - goal fixed.]**

8. Katniss is injured but not as severely as Gale. Katniss's mom tends to Gale's wounds. Peeta tends to Katniss, and Haymitch supports everyone. The threat to Gale's life brings clarity to Katniss's feelings for him.

9. **Key Scene # 3 - First Pinch Point 33%.** Katniss dreams of the games. She awakes confused and at first wishes that Peeta was present to comfort her, but he is tending to Gale. Katniss talks with Haymitch about next steps. The square has been transformed with propaganda banners and machine guns. **They watch as the Hob is burned to the ground.** Katniss realizes that starting a revolution maybe more dangerous than she thought. Katniss receives her wedding dresses and freaks out. She heads for the forest to collect her thoughts. Katniss encounters a woman who has a cracker with the mockingjay stamped on it. **[Force of opposition is shown.]**

10. PART 2. Katniss speaks with the two runaways from District 8. They describe the failed attempted rebellion in their district and their escape. They plan on going to District 13 and tell Katniss she remains their one hope. She heads back but is trapped on the wrong side of the fence when it is electrified.

11. **Key Scene #4 - Twist #1.** Katniss is forced to jump from a tree and suffers a broken tailbone and other injuries. Katniss arrives home limping and is met by her mother, Prim, Peeta, Haymitch, and two peacekeepers that have a message from the head of law enforcement. Katniss is tended to by her mother and sent to bed. Days go by as she heals, but she sees on the news confirmation that **District 13 just might exist.**

12. **Key Scene #5 – Midpoint.** The prep team arrives at Katniss's house for the photo shoot of Katniss in her wedding dresses. The two rebel leaders exchange information and plot the future. Katniss realizes once again that a rebellion is hard work. Caesar and Cinna host a TV show that is mandatory viewing throughout the country. The pictures of Katniss in her wedding dresses are broadcast to an adoring nation. The Quarter Quell ritual is described by Snow. **Katniss realizes she and Peeta will have to go back into the arena for another battle [Everything now changes].**

13. Katniss escapes and ends up in Haymitch's house, where they drink. Haymitch and Katniss make a pact to keep Peeta alive. A drunken Katniss returns to her home and finds Gale there. Gale understands that the Capitol intends to kill her. Katniss feels engulfed in hopelessness. She, Haymitch, and Peeta start training again. The reaping takes place as their names are announced. They're all put on the train and leave District 12.

14. Katniss mourns the fact that she was given no time to say good-bye. She and Peeta hug, the team reviews the reaping results. There are short descriptions of some of the Tributes.

15. Cinna once again comes up with ingenious outfits for Katniss and Peeta to wear for the opening ceremony. They make their grand entrance at the ceremony. Afterward, she meets Chaff and Seeder.

16. Peeta and Katniss arrive at their old quarters and realize that one of the peacekeepers from District 12 has been turned into a mute Avox—a reminder of the power of the Capitol. The team discusses strategies, and all teams practice. For Katniss's "talent,"

she makes a noose and hangs a dummy of Seneca Crane, the former game maker who had been forced to kill himself.

17. The team discusses what just happened, and Peeta reveals he painted a picture of Rue, which is also certain to upset the powers that be. Katniss spends the day with Peeta, then they dress for the spotlight. Katniss is forced to wear one of the wedding dresses, which causes an emotional uproar. Then the dress bursts into "flames" and turns into a mockingjay with feathers and wings, further taunting the Capitol.

18 **Key Scene #6 - Pinch Point #2 - 66% Mark. In** his interview on stage with Caesar, Peeta says he and Katniss already married in secret. Then he says Katniss is pregnant. This emotional shocker moves all the victors from all districts to hold hands and sway. **The whole nation is in an uproar.** Katniss, after spending the night with Peeta, is prepped for the games by Cinna. When she is in the launch tube, she watches in horror as **Cinna is beat up and dragged away [The opposition is encroaching on her].**

19. PART 3. Katniss, shocked, has to focus. She is surrounded by water. The games begin. She swims to the cornucopia. Finnick is there as she grabs a bow, but he assures her he's her ally. They kill a few, Finnick goes to help Peeta, then grabs old Mags. Peeta runs into a force field and appears dead.

20. **75% Mark.** Finnick gives Peeta CPR, and he comes to. They move on, Katniss flinging nuts at the force field to locate it. Katniss climbs a tree, sees the arena is a perfect wheel. They make camp, and the sky lights up with the showing of the dead Tributes. A parachute drops a metal object, and Katniss IDs it as a stile to push into a tree trunk to get sap. This allays their dangerous thirst. They sleep, a bell rings twelve times, it rains, then acid fog seeps in.

21. **Build to the Climax.** They run from the acid fog, which debilitates their limbs. Finnick and Katniss carry Peeta and Mags, but they fail. Mags dies. The fog dissipates. They reach the water and soak in it. She and Peeta drag Finnick in. Monkeys attack and

they fight. Just as Peeta is about to be killed, the morphling from District 6 blocks him and takes the attack on herself.

22. **Key Scene #7 - Twist #2.** Peeta stabs the monkey. The girl dies. A parachute floats down with much-needed ointment. Another cannon blast signals another death. They hide as they spot three Tributes coming. It's Johanna and two others to join them. Wiress keeps saying "tick tock," and Katniss realizes the arena is a clock, divided into twelve sections.

23. They realize specific dangers begin in each section at their specific time. So now they know how to avoid the dangers. They're attacked, and Wiress and two Tributes die. The land spins and they're flung. Katniss swims to grab the coil of wire from Wiress's hands before her body is hauled up into the sky. Katniss realizes some of the victors are trying to keep Peeta alive. Then she hears a scream that sounds like her sister, Prim.

24. Katniss runs, then finds a jabberjay and realizes that was what she heard. Finnick runs after another scream. They see Peeta and Johanna but they're mute, on the other side of an invisible barrier. Katniss and Finnick drop to the ground as they hear the "cries" of their loved ones, then the torment ends, and Peeta assures Katniss their families can't be dead. Another cannon. A parachute with rolls to eat. Peeta and Katniss talk about who should survive and why.

25. The next day Katniss teaches Peeta how to swim. Beetee comes up with a plan to electrocute the remaining opponents. Katniss leads the way to the force field. Peeta finds a pearl in an oyster and gives it to her. They wait.

26. **Key Scene #8 - Dark Night leading to the Climax.** Beetee unrolls the wire. They're to run it down to the water. Katniss and Johanna start off, but someone has cut the wire. They're attacked. Katniss is hit in the head. Johanna digs with her knife into Katniss's arm. She thinks Johanna means to kill her and worries for Peeta. Finnick runs by. The cannon booms. She thinks everyone is hunting her and Peeta. Everything looks hopeless. She

winds Beetee's wire around her arrow and shoots it into the dome. An explosion rocks the world.

27. **Key Scene #9 Climax – No Resolution Scene #10 – hanging ending to lead into next book.** Katniss thinks everyone is dead and all is lost. A hovercraft appears above her. She's hoisted into the vehicle, thinks this is the end for her, and blacks out. She finally wakes and sets off in search of Peeta. She heads down the hall, hears voices speaking in a room, realizes Finnick and Haymitch are in conversation. She bursts in, and they fill her in on what really happened during the game. An underground movement protected her and arranged her escape. She is the mockingjay, and the rebellion needs her. And they are on their way to District 13. She learns Peeta's been captured. Gale shows up and assures Katniss her family is safe, but District 12 is no more. **[Huge development of bigger stakes, bigger commitment.]**

Now, take a look at the same chart as I identify what I would consider the next layer. As I showed you in the previous chart, **scenes 11–20 are in boldface** to make them easier to spot.

If I had written this book, I would have started my plotting with those ten key scenes, then come up with the next layer using the action-reaction method. Who knows how Suzanne Collins plotted her story, but I hope you can see how this might be a logical way to do it.

* * *

1. Setup. Katniss reflects on the changes to her life since arriving back from the Hunger Games. She brings food to Gale's family and spreads her wealth around. She reinforces her relationship with Haymitch, waking him from his liquor-induced slumber. Peta arrives with bread. Katniss's uncertainty regarding her feelings for Peta is evident.

2. **Scene #11 – Twist and complication.** President Snow shows up at Katniss's house. He indicates he would have preferred her (and Peta's) death at the end of the Hunger Games as he grills Katniss. The conflict/stakes are established as high as ever.

3. **Scene #12 - Katniss processes what just happened**. She attempts to make sense out of her exchange with President Snow while she bathes in preparation for her prep team's arrival. The trio arrives to prepare Katniss for her tour of the districts. Katniss is encouraged to develop a talent. Peta and Katniss exchange a kiss before the cameras. Haymitch tells her she will never have a real life—the one she wants with Gale.

4. Inciting Incident. On the train, Katniss details the recent visit with President Snow to her team. She runs through her next moves and options. Effie and Katniss eat breakfast on their "travel day" before arriving at District 11. Peeta shows her his paintings. They arrive at District 11 and do their act. Peeta offers the district a portion of their winnings. Then Katniss speaks consolingly to the crowd. They show solidarity with the mockingjay salute. Katniss realizes she's unleashed the whirlwind and in horror watches a man shot because of her.

5. **Scene #13 – Reaction.** They hurry back into the Justice building as more shots are fired. Haymitch demands to know what happened. Peeta explodes in guilt. Quick montage as they spend days doing the same appearances at all the other districts, until they arrive at the capitol, where they make their final appearance before Snow.

6. **Scene #14 – New twist, raised stakes.** They attend the big party at Snow's mansion. Katniss thinks about the suffering people. Scene ends with her seeing a secret transmission showing **a violent uprising in District 8.**

7. Flashback: Katniss is in the woods on her way to the cabin for a rendezvous with Gale. Gale and Katniss draw closer, and Gale announces his love for her. Katniss tells Gale about the uprising in District 8. Gale reacts strongly to this information. Katniss tells of her plan to run away. They argue about options, the world predicament. Coming out of the woods, Katniss seeks out Peeta to explain her plan and seek his approval. Gale is whipped in the square for his transgression of hunting in the forest. [THIS IS ALSO THE 25% MARK-GOAL FIXED]

8. **SCENE #15 – Reaction.** Katniss is injured but not as severely as Gale. Katniss's mom tends to Gale's wounds. Peeta tends to Katniss and Haymitch supports everyone. **The threat to Gale's life brings clarity to Katniss's feelings for him.**

9. First Pinch Point 33%. Katniss dreams of the games. She awakes confused and at first wishes that Peeta was present to comfort her but he is tending to Gale. Katniss talks with Haymitch about next steps. The square has been transformed with propaganda banners and machine guns. They watch as the Hob is burned to the ground. Katniss realizes that starting a revolution maybe more dangerous than she thought. Katniss receives her wedding dresses and freaks out. She heads for the forest to collect her thoughts. Katniss encounters a woman who has a cracker with the mockingjay stamped on it. [FORCE OF OPPOSITION IS SHOWN]

10. **SCENE #16 – New development.** PART 2 Katniss speaks with the two runaways from District 8. They describe the failed attempted rebellion in their district and their escape. They plan on going to District 13 and tell Katniss she remains their one hope. She heads back but is trapped on the wrong side of the fence when it is electrified.

11. Twist #1. Katniss is forced to jump from a tree and suffers a broken tailbone and other injuries. Katniss arrives home limping and is met by her mother, Prim, Peeta, and Haymitch, and two peacekeepers that have a message from the head of law enforcement. Katniss is tended to by her mother and sent to bed. Days go by as she heals, but she sees on the news confirmation that District 13 just might exist

12. Midpoint. The prep team arrives at Katniss's house for the photo shoot of Katniss in her wedding dresses. The two rebel leaders exchange information and plot the future. Katniss realizes once again that a rebellion is hard work. Caesar and Cinna host a TV show that is mandatory viewing throughout the country. The pictures of Katniss in her wedding dresses are broadcast to an adoring nation. The Quarter Quell ritual is described by Snow.

Katniss realizes she and Peeta will have to go back into the arena for another battle [EVERYTHING NOW CHANGES].

13. Katniss escapes and ends up in Haymitch's house where they drink. Haymitch and Katniss make a pack to keep Peeta alive. A drunken Katniss returns to her home and finds Gale there. Gale understands that the Capitol intends to kill her. Katniss feels engulfed in hopelessness. She, Haymitch, and Peeta start training again. The reaping takes place as their names are announced. They're all put on the train and leave District 12.

14. Katniss mourns the fact that she was given no time to say good-bye. She and Peeta hug, the team reviews the reaping results. There are short descriptions of some of the Tributes.

15. Cinna once again comes up with ingenious outfits for Katniss and Peeta to wear for the opening ceremony. They make their grand entrance at the ceremony. Afterward, she meets Chaff and Seeder.

16. **SCENE #17 – Twist.** Peeta and Katniss arrive at their old quarters and realize that one of the peacekeepers from District 12 has been turned into a mute Avox—a reminder of the power of the capitol. The team discusses strategies and all teams practice. For Katniss's "talent," she makes a noose and hangs a dummy of Seneca Crane, the former game maker who had been forced to kill himself. **[Shows Katniss raising the stakes]**

17. **SCENE #18 – Twist.** The team discusses what just happened, and Peeta reveals he painted a picture of Rue, which is also certain to upset the powers that be. Katniss spends the day with Peeta, then they dress for the spotlight. Katniss is forced to wear one of the wedding dresses, which causes an emotional uproar. Then the dress bursts into "flames" and turns into **a mockingjay** with feathers and wings. **[Raises the stakes even higher.]**

18 66% Mark – Pinch Point #2. in his interview on stage with Caesar, Peeta says he and Katniss already married in secret. Then he says Katniss is pregnant. This emotional shocker moves all the victors from all districts to hold hands and sway. The whole nation is in an uproar. Katniss, after spending the night with Peeta, is prepped

for the games by Cinna. When she is in the launch tube, she watches in horror as Cinna is beat up and dragged away [The opposition is encroaching on her].

19. Part 3. Katniss, shocked, has to focus. She is surrounded by water. The games begin. She swims to the cornucopia. Finnick is there as she grabs a bow. But he assures her he's her ally. They kill a few, Finnick goes to help Peeta, then grabs old Mags. Peeta runs into a force field and appears dead.

20. 75% MARK. Finnick gives Peeta CRP and he comes to. They move on, Katniss flinging nuts at the force field to delineate it. Katniss climbs a tree, sees the arena is a perfect wheel. They make camp and the sky lights up with the showing of the dead Tributes. A parachute drops a metal object, and Katniss IDs it as a stile to push into a tree trunk to get sap. This allays their dangerous thirst. They sleep, a bell rings twelve times, it rains, then acid fog seeps in.

21. Build to the Climax. They run from the acid fog, which debilitates their limbs. Finnick and Katniss carry Peeta and Mags, but they fail. Mags dies. The fog dissipates. They reach the water and soak in it. She and Peeta drag Finnick in. Monkeys attack and they fight. Just as Peeta is about to be killed, the morphling from District 6 blocks him and takes the attack on herself.

22. Twist #2. Peeta stabs the monkey. The girl dies. A parachute floats down with much-needed ointment. Another cannon blast signals another death. They hide as they spot three Tributes coming. It's Johanna and two others to join them. Wiress keeps saying "tick tock" and Katniss realizes the arena is a clock, divided into twelve sections.

23. **SCENE #19 – Important realizations and developments.** They realize specific dangers begin in each section at their specific time. **So now they know how to avoid the dangers.** They're attacked and Wiress and two Tributes die. The land spins and they're flung. Katniss swims to **grab the coil of wire from Wiress's hands** before she's hauled up into the sky. **Katniss**

realizes some of the victors are trying to keep Peeta alive.
Then she hears a scream that sounds like her sister, Prim.

24. Katniss runs, then finds a jabberjay and realizes that was what she heard. Finnick runs after another scream. They see Peeta and Johanna but they're mute, on the other side of an invisible barrier. Katniss and Finnick drop to the ground as they hear the "cries" of their loved ones, the torment ends, and Peeta assures Katniss their families can't be dead. Another cannon. A parachute with rolls to eat. Peeta and Katniss talks about who should survive and why.

25. **SCENE #20 – Key development.** The next day Katniss teaches Peeta how to swim. Beetee comes up with a **plan to electrocute** the remaining opponents. Katniss leads the way to the force field. Peeta finds a pearl in an oyster and gives it to her. They wait. **[Sets up the action in the climax with the roll of wire.]**

26. Key Scene #8 Dark Night leading to the Climax. Beetee unrolls the wire. They're to run it down to the water. Katniss and Johanna start off but someone has cut the wire. They're attacked. Katniss is hit in the head. Johanna digs with her knife into Katniss's arm. She thinks Johanna means to kill her and worries for Peeta. Finnick runs by. The cannon booms. She thinks everyone is hunting her and Peeta. Everything looks hopeless. She winds Beetee's wire around her arrow and shoots it into the dome. An explosion rocks the world.

27. Key Scene #9 Climax. Katniss thinks everyone is dead and all is lost. A hovercraft appears above her. She's hoisted into the vehicle, sees the face of the game master, thinks this is the end for her and blacks out. She fades in and out, finally waking, and sets off in search of Peeta. She heads down the hall, hears voices speaking in a room. Realizes Finnick and Haymitch are in conversation. She bursts in and they fill her in on what really happened during the game. An underground movement protected her and arranged her escape. She is the mockingjay, and the rebellion needs her. And they are on their way to District 13. She learns Peeta's been captured. Gale shows up and assures Katniss her family is safe, but District 12 is no more. [Huge development of bigger stakes, bigger commitment.]

* * *

You may have chosen different key scenes for your second layer. I chose those next ten scenes not because they were the next ten *most important* scenes. Rather, I focused on *reaction, processing, and new action.*

Inexperienced writers often have a lot of useless scenes in their novels, and most of those fall in the middle. To avoid that middle slump, layering scenes that show *immediate reaction* to what just happened, leading to *processing and decisive new action* is the way to go.

A story is about characters who act, then react to what just happened. Action-reaction-processing-decision-new action. Some novels have myriad developments, as you see in *Catching Fire* and other high-stakes dramas. Others have few plot developments.

Regardless, you can't go wrong if you have a balance of action, processing, and reaction scenes.

I hope you can see how, once you add the layer of the second set of ten scenes, that paves the way for the next layer of ten scenes. Take a look at the remaining scenes in this last chart. Guess what? We see more processing, new developments and twists, complications and raised stakes.

Once the goal is set at the quarter mark, everything from there is building to the climax with higher stakes, greater obstacles, stronger opposition, and messier complications. That's solid story structure.

This chapter showed you how you might layer your novel focusing on the natural action-reaction process. But if you have a great subplot (or are considering developing one), you might want to make that the focus of your second layer of scenes.

Let's take a look at how that might be done.

* * *

Your assignment: Grab a favorite book (best seller) in the genre you are writing, then summarize every scene in the book as shown in the *Catching Fire* example. Go through and identify the ten key scenes (mark them in bold and number them). Then go through that list of scenes again and find the next layer of ten scenes—by looking for reaction and new action.

Notice how the author placed "processing" scenes after an important plot development. Notice scenes that showcase new action based on a decision made via that processing. This will help you see how you might create your second layer for your novel.

Chapter 11: Layering a Subplot into Your Novel

Let's talk a moment about subplots.

When I started writing novels, I had no clue about subplots. I figured my books needed them, but I didn't know why. And without knowing why I should include a subplot into my story, I didn't have the insights needed to craft one.

Not every novel has one or needs one, and genre often determines this. With many high-action suspense-thrillers, there is just the one plot, with the protagonist chasing after that specific goal. Many subgenres of romance omit subplots; the story is focused on the guy getting the gal and little else.

But regardless of genre, I believe just about any novel will benefit by a strong subplot or two.

Oddly, to me, there isn't much written about subplots, but subplots are everywhere. We see them in the movies we watch, and they are in many novels we read. We may instinctively know how they work in story structure. I always thought they were inserted to give some depth to the overall story, whether movie or novel. And that is one purpose for a subplot.

But writers need to be careful not to throw any ol' subplot into a story with the hope that it will merely add some interest. If you keep in mind that everything that goes into your novel must serve the advancement and complication of the main plot, you will fare well.

Subplots Serve a Purpose

What do I mean by "serve the advancement" of the main plot? The main plot is all about a protagonist going after a goal in the midst of conflict and high stakes. That's the essence of the main plot's purpose—to be a vehicle for this character and her objective in the story.

So, if you keep in mind that any subplots (additional plotlines) you create should add to the main plot in a meaningful way, that can help you come up with some interesting and helpful subplots.

Subplots are also great vehicles to bring out themes and motifs. A subplot situation could present another side to a theme of justice or ignorance or forgiveness.

Subplots can involve your protagonist and/or your secondary characters. Regardless, whatever side story you weave into your novel, it needs to impact your protagonist.

I have read numerous novels, some by best-selling authors, who have thrown subplots into their stories that don't fit at all. These subplots feel dropped in as noise and distraction, and I've sometimes found myself skimming pages to get past them in order to get back to the gripping main plot. That's a bad thing.

In addition to being irrelevant to the novel's purpose and premise, they are often boring, highlighting mundane concerns and activities that don't add anything of interest. And that makes for a dissatisfied reader.

Do you need a subplot in your novel? You may not have thought much about this, but I hope this exploration into layering in a subplot will spark some ideas for you.

We first need to look at why a subplot might enhance a novel. And here's my simple answer: if you want your novel to reflect a slice of real life in some way (whether a "realistic" story or a fantasy), subplots will add to that sense of realism or believability.

Plot Layers

The "plot" of our life is loaded with subplots. I find it helps to think about plot in layers. And since this book is all about layering your novel's scenes, this layering concept ties in nicely.

Plot layers come in all thicknesses of importance, and if they are designed carefully, they will make your story a rich one with unique and lasting flavors that will linger long after your reader finishes your book.

One way that may help you in conceptualizing this is to think about your own life. You have some big goals—long-term, long-range goals, or maybe even just one—on the horizon at the moment. Maybe it's to finish college and get that degree. Maybe it's to start a family and create your dream life with your spouse.

In a novel, that might equate to your main plot, which features the visible goal your protagonist is trying to reach. This is the overarching plot that all the other plot layers will sit under. But just as with a multilayer cake, when you take that bite, the different flavors of the layers should complement one another and create a delightful overall taste. I wouldn't want to bite into a layer of catsup in my chocolate cake.

As that "plot" plays out in your life, other things encroach or dovetail into that goal. You may be dealing with some personal issue—such as a recurring health problem or a former boyfriend who keeps showing up against your wishes. You may also be dealing with trivial things, such as trying to decide what color to paint your bedroom, and the paint store guy, who's completely incompetent, can't get the color right.

Life is complex. It's messy. We're told to complicate our characters' lives. Well, this is the best way to do it—by introducing many layers of plot, and not just for your protagonist but for your secondary characters as well. So it stands to reason that layering in a subplot after your ten key scenes are in place in your outline is a logical next step.

Vary the Intensity of Each Layer

Think about creating three layers (at least), and let's refer to them as plots A, B, and C. You know your A plot—it's the main one driving your story. But now you need B and C.

You want B to be an important layer that will help the main plot along—either something that enhances Plot A or runs headlong into conflict with it.

Plot C will be thinner and more trivial, and may even add that comic relief in your tension (picture your character trying to get the paint guy with myopia to see the obvious difference between the two unmatching paint swatches). Believe it or not, Plot C can serve the purpose of revealing a lot of emotion and character (ever thrown a hissy fit at a store when you're having a bad day because of some bigger concern?).

Take this a step further and imagine one of your secondary, supportive characters in your novel dealing with an issue that juxtaposes with your protagonist's issues. This is what I meant earlier when I said a subplot can enhance and showcase your themes.

What if Ann, your heroine, is fighting infertility, and at her peak of despair at being unable to conceive, her best friend Joan not only learns she's accidentally gotten pregnant but Ann learns she's going in for an abortion. Can you see how this plot layer can add depth to your story by providing a place to reveal more of your protagonist's needs, fears, and personality—as well as create meaningful conflict?

An Example of a Subplot Process

In *A Thin Film of Lies*, a mystery I wrote years ago that needed a big revision, I decided to make a secondary character my protagonist.

Fran is a bit sketchy in the original story; you know a little about her life, personality, and tastes. She's the lead homicide detective investigating a hit-and-run, and Mike Jepson, businessman, seems guilty. Evidence mounts to indicate that Jepson ran down Libby with his car, and Mike ends up arrested and in jail, despite his protests that he's innocent (Plot A).

This genre is clear. It's a detective story. So the plot plays out with the development of the investigation of the apparent crime, building to the big climax and twists that reveal "whodunit" and what happens next (surprise twist at the end).

So my challenge was in coming up with a subplot that was just right for my novel. Since my main theme centered on *the protestation of innocence* and Fran's challenge in believing in Jepson's innocence despite the "proof," I decided I would run a parallel subplot with that theme.

I set up that Fran's husband left her, without a warning, ten years earlier, and now her two kids are teens. Trevor is seventeen and struggling emotionally. He is at odds with Mom. But it's more than typical teen angst. That ten-year anniversary of hubby's abandonment is fast approaching, and Fran has never really talked to Trevor about his pain (or hers). Clearly he's having abandonment issues.

This all ties into the rich character arc and spiritual/emotional MDQ I want answered in the novel. Meaning, Fran has not faced her own pain and hurt—not fully—regarding her husband's flight. I decided to use the subplot as a means to set her on this journey so that by the climax, she has to face all the ugliness—her pain and feelings of failure as a parent—through the conflict with Trevor.

Pause for a moment. What I did was use Plot B to play out, for the most part, the character arc. To answer the spiritual MDQ. Something to think about.

So "secondary character" Fran now became my protagonist. Not only did I deepen her involvement with the main plot and increase the number of her scenes, I came up with a subplot that added an ongoing, growing tension with her teenage son that exposed issues of trust and believability—elements that are key themes of my main plot.

Fran doesn't really believe in her perp's claims of innocence, nor does she believe her son's when he insists he didn't hack the school's computer.

I laid out a list of about ten scenes (full and partial) that could develop this subplot. Just as with any main plot, your subplot needs an arc.

Let me repeat that, in case you missed it: your subplot needs a story arc too.

There's an introductory or setup scene that shows the situation (which may or may not already be in progress), followed by numerous scenes that . . . you guessed it—complicate and build the subplot to its big climax.

It was when I layered in this subplot (a few years ago) that I got that "aha moment" regarding layering. It was so easy to first create a summary of those ten subplot scenes, write them (back to back in one document, for cohesion), then insert each scene in the proper place in my earlier novel draft. Which might be something for you to consider doing.

You can either chart out your novel with the subplot scenes before you begin writing, or you can write your first draft, then write all your subplot scenes, then insert those scenes in just the right places in your story. Make sense?

Let me say this: it's a whole lot of fun to do.

The Beauty of Subplot C

In those subplot scenes (Plot B) in my crime novel, I also included *brief* moments dealing with Plot C.

Brief is the operative word here.

Since Plot C elements are usually minor, they aren't going to take up a lot of space in your novel. Though, having that big "fall apart" scene at the paint store could be an important development in your story.

But . . . if you spend dozens of pages and multiple scenes on insignificant action in your novel (Plot C), you are going to bore readers and waste valuable space.

I had already set the novel in Los Angeles in the heat of summer, so it was logical to create a Plot C that tied in with that. In the midst of Fran dealing with her "son" issues, I had her hate the LA heat and gave her terrible asthma, so my Plot C is the aggravating element of her air conditioner at home always going on the fritz—which compounds and exacerbates the tension and "heat" in her house and family life. And I found a way, at a key moment near the climax, to bring in some symbolism (about things always breaking and not being able to fix everything in life . . .) through that Plot C.

In my latest novel, I wanted to give my character Seasonal Affective Disorder (SAD) in order to compound her health and emotional issues, so I set the novel in the Pacific Northwest, in a region where it's gray and rainy much of the year.

So while you're playing with your plot and scene ideas and trying to come up with subplots, think about exterior elements that could come into play, especially with your Plot C.

Play with your themes; find places in your novel, or create new scenes, where you can bring these themes to the forefront. If you do, you will end up with a delicious, irresistible story readers will love.

Complicate Matters

The secret to crafting great subplots is found in this word: *complicate*. If you make it your objective to use your subplots to complicate your story, that is a first strong construction step.

That doesn't mean you want to throw in side stories that are only messy situations, though.

The best purpose for subplots is to enrich, deepen, and help advance the main plot and reveal character motivation. So with every subplot you add in (and often, the more the better), utilizing any number of secondary characters, find a way for this additional story line to be a complication.

For whom? Ultimately, for your protagonist. For, even if the subplot is about another character, the impact of what that character is going through has to affect your protagonist (unless you are dealing with multiple timelines and the characters never interact).

Don't throw random subplots into your novel just for filler or because you think they are neat ideas. They really must serve a purpose in your story. Sure, make them entertaining or provide comic relief. Subplots help to bring out your characters and all their issues, and they can be a vehicle for making your characters clash, which, to me, is the best reason for layering plots.

Creating That Subplot Layer

Since subplots are common to novels, it's only natural that creating a second layer that builds the subplot would come in handy. Writers probably don't step back and consider how many scenes should be devoted to the subplot (or subplots) and where they might be inserted in the story. I've read novels in which the subplot is glomped in the middle of the book or crammed into the second half of the novel.

A strong subplot should be carefully plotted for best impact. As I mentioned, I believe a subplot should act in tandem with the primary plot, building in importance, intensity, and in impact. Even if it's a small subplot, if it ties in with the novel's themes and provides key information at key times, it's worthy of a layer.

In *A Thin Film of Lies*, note that the situation regarding the subplot (the trouble with Trevor) is mentioned and thought about in many other scenes as Fran mulls her problems over in her mind or discusses with coworkers or friends. But the actual *full scenes* in which the subplot plays out comprises six big scenes.

I came up with a subplot that involves Trevor being accused of hacking into the school's computer and changing some grades of some of the students. Trevor claims he's innocent, but evidence strongly proves he's guilty.

I mentioned that I wrote all the subplot scenes in a separate document, back to back. This is extremely helpful because you avoid any disjointedness or clunky flow from one scene to the next. It's almost as if you are writing a mini novel on the side that you then break up into pieces and insert into your story.

When I wrote *The Hidden Kingdom*, I used a story within a story, so I did this exact thing. All the scenes with Alia and her husband and son on another planet were written in a separate document. I had five full scenes, which included the opening and closing scenes of the novel. In these scenes, Alia is basically telling the plot of the novel to her son as a bedtime story. But these are detailed scenes, not just short excerpts. By using this same method of layering, I was able to achieve, with ease, the effect I intended and found it a perfect way to keep continuity and flow.

What then? Once you've written all those scenes and you've created a kind of mini novel with your subplot (because you will have a beginning, middle, climax, and ending), you determine where to place each scene.

Here's the list of subplot scenes I created and where I placed them in *A Thin Film of Lies*. Remember: the elements connected to the subplot can come out in dialogue and thought in small bits *throughout* the book, and should, because your character, while at work or play, will be thinking about this important Plot B in her life. But these noted in the chart are full scenes, which you need with strong subplots.

Before the first full subplot scene, I've set up that Fran is having issues with her teenage son, Trevor. We've met him and witnessed this, and seen Fran's worry over him. I've noted in parentheses where each scene falls in the novel.

Chapter 11 (35% mark): Fran goes as chaperone on a class trip with her son. At the park, she stumbles upon a drug sale gone violent that involves a couple of Trevor's classmates and intervenes. Trevor is angry and embarrassed at her mother's cop actions.

Chapter 15 (52%): Fran is called into school. Trevor is in the principal's office, accused of hacking the school's computers to change grades. He swears he's innocent but evidence proves otherwise. Parallels Fran's case, with Jepson arrested for hit-and-run and swearing he's innocent. [We later see a short bit showing

Fran has scheduled an IT expert to go to the school and investigate the claim.]

Chapter 16 (58%) Fran plays softball with coworkers. Reveals the backstory about her marriage, her husband leaving without a word ten years ago, that ten-year anniversary looming and how it ties in with her disconnect with Trevor, how she's tried to be the best mom but feels she's failed.

Chapter 18 (65%): Fran is home. Daughter Megan arrives distraught. Her boyfriend broke up with her, and she feels she's unlovable. This unleashes Fran's insecurities and loneliness, and emphasizes Fran's need to be perfect and please everyone, never make a mistake. Which is key in this subplot with Trevor.

Chapter 19 (71%): Fran finds Trevor at the park. She tries to talk to him. She has good news—turns out, due to her efforts, that evidence proves Trevor was set up (just like Jepson). He gets angry—she didn't believe he was innocent even though he insisted he was. He accuses her of not having faith in him. She mentions that his dad leaving is at the heart of all his pain. He feels like he's a loser and confesses that he believes that's why Dad left. Then he storms off. This starts Fran's descent into emotional darkness. [Note how this Plot B element follows a similar story structure as does the main plot.]

(95%): After the main plot climax, Fran leaves the final crime scene and arrives home with blood on her clothes. Trevor freaks at the sight, and Fran is feeling completely vulnerable. Today is the tenth anniversary of her husband leaving. Fran and Trevor have the healing heart-to-heart when Fran breaks down, blames herself for hubby leaving, for being a terrible mom, and realizes she's tried to be the perfect mom and that her efforts have backfired. What her kids need is for her to fail, to be imperfect. Fran has her big epiphany and faces her greatest inner fear. They finally talk about Dad for the first time, and healing results.

Note that the subplot resolves *after* the main plot is resolved in the climax. Both plot goals (Jepson and Trevor exonerated for their supposed crimes) resolve, but it's in *this* scene, with the subplot, that

Fran's *spiritual* MDQ is answered, and her character arc comes to completion.

In other words, Fran solves the police case at the climax, but when she leaves for home after it's all over, the subplot needs to wrap up.

Yes, I had the visible plot sealed with Trevor's innocence proven back at that 70% mark (that case now closed), but the *actual* subplot—which is really about Fran's relationship with her son—doesn't resolve until the end of the novel.

I hope you see how adding this rich subplot gives my novel depth and showcases the themes.

There are many ways you might weave in a subplot, and the number of scenes you have may vary, but here's a basic way you could layer that second set of ten scenes. (I'm going to put them in order as they appear in the novel but keep the numbering based on the layering system, so the subplot layer scenes are 11-20, as I did with *Catching Fire*.)

Chart: The Subplot Second Layer

#1 Setup. Introduce protagonist in her world. Establish her core need. Set the stage, begin building the world, bring key characters on stage.

#11 **Introduction of subplot.** Set up the situation between the characters to show the existing tension and attitudes that is causing conflict.

#2 Turning Point #1 (10%) Inciting Incident.

#12 **Show how the Inciting Incident affects the subplot.** It may trigger it, bring it to the forefront. Have something initially happen with the subplot to bring in problems and complications.

#3 Pinch Point #1 (33% roughly). Give a glimpse of the opposition's power, need, and goal as well as the stakes.

#13 **New subplot development that mirrors or is opposite of the main plot.** In other words, show what key opposition your protagonist is facing and how she feels about it (a mirroring pinch point, in essence).

#4 Twist #1. Something new happens: a new ally, a friend becomes a foe. New info reveals a serious complication to reaching the goal. Protagonist must adjust to change with this setback.

#14 **Progress with the subplot.** Similar to the main plot, the character is trying to deal with the subplot issues, complications, and setbacks. Tension builds as things are getting more difficult or problematic.

#5 The Midpoint (50%). No turning back. Important event that propels the story forward and solidifies the protagonist's determination to reach her goal.

#15 **Things start coming to a head and creating high tension** with the subplot. Now that the protagonist is committed to going all-in after her goal, the subplot adds stress to her load.

#6 Pinch Point #2 (62% roughly). The opposition comes full force. Time to buckle down and fight through it.

#16 Developments with the subplot reach critical mass. Things are falling apart, looking hopeless.

#7 Twist 2. An unexpected surprise giving (false?) hope. The goal now looks within reach. A mentor gives encouragement, a secret weapon, or an important clue.

#17 Subplot feels at a standstill. Protagonist has no time to deal with it, and so this creates more tension. Or something in the subplot could provide the help, insight, clue the protagonist needs to push harder to the goal.

#8 Turning Point #4 (75%) Major setback. All is lost and hopeless. Time for final push.

#18 Same issues with the subplot. Seems unresolvable. Something happens that closes doors. Or the subplot might be resolved outwardly, but the desired emotional state is elusive.

#9 Turning Point #5 (76-99%). The climax in which the goal is either reached or not; the two MDQs are answered.

#19 The key scene that resolves the subplot in a completely satisfying, full way. The character has achieved the emotional resolution she's wanted from the start.

#10 The aftermath (90-99%). The wrap-up at the end. Dénouement, resolution.

#20 A final, parting shot of the result of the subplot wrapped up. This could be included in the last scene (above) as the two plot elements merge together, or they might be separate scenes within the final chapter(s).

Note, too, that the subplot may not directly be about your protagonist. You may have a dual-protagonist story, as you find in some romance novels. So the subplot could be all about the love interest, or a secondary character. But keep in mind: every subplot should serve the needs of your main plot and impact the protagonist as she goes after her visible goal for the novel.

Also keep in mind that when you get to the end, once the plot and subplot have been resolved fully, you want to end your novel. Remember: "Get in quickly; get out quickly." Tie up all the loose ends, bring the cast of characters on stage, wrap it all up in a nice package in a tight, concise way (whether immediately after the climax in time, or in an epilogue of sorts a few weeks or months later).

But don't drag out your ending. These last scenes are going to be short and sweet, preceding those two wonderful words: *The End.*

Play around with this. You might not intersperse each of the second ten scenes (subplot scenes) so evenly in this way. You might have two back-to back scenes and then nothing for a while. It really depends on your main plot.

But the idea is to drop in those backstory scenes every so often in key places and build to the climax of the subplot as you build to the climax of the main plot.

So first work out a strong subplot that amplifies the themes of your novel, then create an outline of scenes, and maybe even write those scenes. Try writing them in a separate document, then, when you're ready, carefully read through your novel and see where to insert those scenes. You may need to add a few more, or add in a few lines here and there in other scenes to prepare for what's to come or for smooth transitions.

If you can think of a great novel with a great subplot, consider going through that same exercise of summarizing all the scenes, then identifying layer one, then layer two—the subplot layer. You may get some great ideas from this exercise.

We've looked at second layers based on action-reaction and subplots. Now we're going to delve into the romance genre, which has its own special needs.

* * *

Your assignment: Even if you're not sure you want or need a subplot in your novel, play around with developing one. First, jot down your themes or big issues in your novel. Think about your secondary characters and how their views clash with those of your protagonist. Brainstorm a subplot for either your protagonist or a significant secondary character that will either bring out your theme or create great conflict or both.

Make a list of possible scenes, keeping in mind the need to move from setup to climax to resolution. Use the Subplot Layer Chart as a reference to help you figure out what kind of scenes you need and where they go in your novel, then write a one-paragraph summary for each scene. Like what you've done? Use it!

Chapter 12: Layering a Romance

In this chapter I'm going to show you how you can layer the second set of ten scenes in a romance novel (scenes 11-20). Maybe you don't write romance, but don't skip ahead just yet. There are some useful elements to structuring romance novels that you may want to incorporate in your fantasy novel or thriller.

Many popular movies of various genres have that "romance" subplot. Ones that come to mind are *Outbreak*, *Armageddon*, *Speed*, *Star Wars*, and on the list goes.

In other words, don't pooh-pooh romance. Real life includes romance, and many novels can benefit by a romance component. And hey, more than 50 percent of all ebook sales are romance novels. Just sayin' . . .

What's Different about the Romance Journey

We looked at a method in the last chapter that showed you how you can build on your ten foundational scenes by layering with your key subplot. And you can use that method with a romance novel or any other genre, I believe.

But there are some important things to understand about romance novels—the primary thing being the romance story engine.

Think of it this way: most novels have one engine that drives the story (think of a train or car). There is one primary focus or plot the protagonist is involved with.

But with a romance thread, you have two engines, like my hybrid car. You still have the overarching plot or story line. But you also have a romance engine. And while romance, like any other genre, can vary in large degrees, the primary "lover's journey" that you find in romance novels follows a basic structure.

So while the plot is happening, the lovers are meeting, pulling apart and/or being pulled apart, coming together finally at the climax, and earning their HEA (happily ever after) at the end.

Consider Driving Your Romance with a Subplot

With straight romance genre, there is just the one romance engine driving the story. But what can make it a strong story is that developed subplot acting as a force for and against the lovers.

I had to learn well this story structure when I sat down to plot out and write my first historical Western romance, *Colorado Promise.*

I'd had romantic elements and subplots in some of my novels (*Time Sniffers, The Map across Time, The Unraveling of Wentwater*), and some of them were intrinsic to the main plot. But those novels aren't considered romance genre. They don't fit that category, and they wouldn't meet those readers' expectations if I called them romance novels.

So in this chapter I'm going to start to lay out those next ten scene types and show how a romance novel might be structured to work with the secondary story engine—the romance engine.

Because many romance novels alternate between the hero's and the heroine's POV, this may seem like a no-brainer. Again, there are lots of ways you can do this, but I'll show you one example. Your novel idea might call for some variation. And with a first-person novel, this of course is going to be different.

What the "Lover's Journey" Is All About

Before we dig into that romance layer, let's look a bit at the "Lover's Journey" as so wonderfully explained by Hollywood screenwriting consultant Michael Hauge.

According to Hauge, there are some key differences between the classic "hero's journey" and the "lovers' journey." Without going into volumes, let's just say that the modern romance structure follows a specific development, and the bulk of the key scenes are in the last third of the story (he uses the three-act structure because that's common to screenplays).

Take a look at these two charts so you can compare the two journeys.

The Deep Story Hero's Journey Plot Grid:

I Setup (1-2)	II New Situation (3-4)	III Progress (5-6)	IV Complications & Higher Stakes (7-8)	V Final Push (9-11)	VI Reward (12)
Plot Point #1: Opportunity	Turning Change	Point #1 of Plans	Turning Pt#2 Point of No Return	Plot Major	Point #2 Setback	Turning Point #3 Climax

Act I   Act II   Act III

Now the Hero's Journey (Plotline and Grid) to the Standard Romance Story Plot:

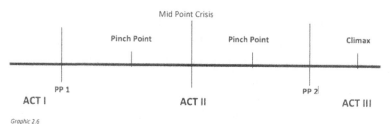

Graphic 2.6

The Deep Story Romance/Lovers' Journey Plot Grid:

1 Opening Sequence (1-2)	2 Central Idea (3-4)	3 Obstacles (5-6)	4 Overcoming (7-8)	5 Close (9-11) (12)

Act I   Act II   Act III

Hauge proposes twelve key scenes in the romance structure. Not every romance story has to have all of these, but they're the milestones you'll see in most romance novels. I often leave out two or three and replace with ones that work better for my story. (NOTE: on the lower chart, those numbers in parentheses pertain to the scene numbers below. In other words, "The Dance"—scene 7—would occur near the end of the much-larger Act II in a romance novel.)

But if you're thinking of writing romance, it will help you to work with these, and I'll show you how these layer in—in general and with specific examples.

Here are the twelve romance scenes (in my wording):

Chart: The 12 Romance Scenes

1. **Ordinary World.** We see the heroine's normal world before she meets the hero.

2. **The Meet.** The lovers meet.

3. **Rebuffed.** Heroine has a negative response to the hero that shows they're incompatible (or make this the hero's reaction to the heroine).

4. **Wise Friend Counsels.** Heroine's friend/mentor points out why the hero is right for her.

5. **Acknowledge Interest.** Heroine is forced to acknowledge her attraction to the hero.

6. **First Quarrel.** Lovers have an argument or disagreement that pushes them apart.

7. **The Dance.** Opposites attract and repel. Development of the relationship but with tension!

8. **The Black Moment.** Romance is dead, impossible due to something that's happened.

9. **The Lovers Reunite.** They finally openly admit/accept they are fated/ meant for each other, but things stand in the way.

10. **Complications Push Them Apart.** Tension leading to the big climax, usually due the complications of the subplot.

11. **Together at Last.** Working together, thrown together, at the climax to overcome the last big obstacle (emotionally and actually), they are finally together or joined in love and purpose.

12. **HEA.** The happily ever after. The reward for the hard journey.

You can probably see how a few of these scenes are going to take the place of some of the ten key scenes (such as #1). Again, this is all flexible, and you can move things around and add in as your plot requires.

With romance stories, the subplot is the ticket because if all you have are scenes showing the hero and heroine talking or walking in the park or arguing over something, you don't have a story.

You need a plot! You need action, secondary characters, and the development of conflict, high stakes, and tension. In other words, you want to throw your hero and heroine into a big situation that can force them to ride that romance engine to the finish line (or train depot).

Layering In Romance Scenes

As I did in previous chapters, I'm going to continue the numbering in bold so you can see where these next ten scenes might be layered over the first ten. Hang in there. This will make sense as we go further.

Take a deep breath and don't get overwhelmed. Pretend this is all fun (because it is!).

NOTE: The 12 key romance scenes are R1, R2, R3, etc.

Also, keep in mind that in many romance novels POVs alternate, so you may have a scene or two in the hero's POV, and then shift to the heroine's. In other words, each of these key scenes could be two halves—a whole scene but one that has a POV shift midway. This is very common with romance novels.

Chart: The Romance Second Layer

#1 (also **R1**) – Setup. Introduce protagonist (heroine) in her world. Establish her core need. Set the stage, begin building the world.

#11 R1 – Introduction of HERO. This is the match to the first essential scene. It may not be the second scene in your novel. You may have two or three scenes with your heroine first. Remember, we're looking a key scenes to lay in as structure—not every single scene.

#2 – Turning Point #1 (10%) Inciting Incident. This incident moves the heroine into position for the meet (a move to another location, an event, etc.).

#12 R2 – The Meet. This may come later. Some say the lovers have to meet in the first scene. I'm not big on that. I want some time to get to know them both before they're thrown together. I want to see their need.

#3 – Pinch Point #1 (33%). Give a glimpse of the opposition's power, need, and goal as well as the stakes. This is the full setup of your subplot, against which your lovers face conflict, opposition, and obstacles.

#13 R4 – Wise Friend Counsels. Again, this can be, and often is, scenes with both the hero and heroine. They can each have a mentor/ally/wise friend character that gives them advice regarding their love life and/or pushing them to consider the potential love interest.

#4 – Twist #1. Something new happens: a new ally, a friend becomes a foe. New info reveals a serious complication to reaching the goal. Protagonist must adjust to change with this setback. With a romance novel, this goal is to reach that HEA, so this leads into . . .

#14 R5 – Acknowledge Interest. A key scene that throws the lovers together so they start getting to really know each other. I often have the twists be disasters (hailstorms, tornados, floods, locust, blizzards, etc.) that have the hero save the heroine (my rule is the hero must save the heroine three times in my novel, the third time the biggie at the climax, so those three "save scenes" are in this ten-scene layer).

#5 – The Midpoint (50%). No turning back. Important event that propels the story forward and solidifies the protagonist's determination to reach her goal. Usually one of the lovers realizes and decides the other is for them, and they will now pursue without letup, despite current obstacles. And at the same time, the other lover may see something that makes him/her decide the relationship is not gonna happen.

#15 R6 – The First Quarrel. Things start coming to a head and creating high tension with the lovers.

#6 – Pinch Point #2 (62%). The opposition comes full force. Time to buckle down and fight through it. Again, this is further development of the subplot. The nemesis or opposition is going to make it nearly impossible for the couple to get together: nature, mean parents, jealous ex, angry former business partner.

#16 R7 – The Dance of Attraction. The two are again thrown together, and now they are perilously close to falling madly in love. But . . . there are still obstacles (subplot unresolved) and emotional resistance due to fear and doubt and past wounds.

#7 – Twist 2. An unexpected surprise giving (false?) hope. The goal now looks within reach. A mentor gives encouragement, a secret weapon, or an important clue. Events occur to make this romance look possible, giving hope. Which causes . . .

#17 R8 – The Black Moment. Then something happens to kill the possibility of a true romance. A misdirection, lie, reversal, misunderstanding. This is a great place to throw in that monkey wrench. A parent announces at a party that the heroine is going to marry choice B, and the hero finds out and thinks all is lost.

#8 – Turning Point #4 (75%). Major setback. All is lost and hopeless. Time for final push. Think about the scene in *Ever After*, when

Prince Henry is wrongly told by his mother the queen (who was lied to by the evil stepmother) that Danielle left France to go marry some other guy. Danielle, for her part, learns that her gig is up and is locked in the pantry, unable to go to the ball. Dark, dark moment of lost hope. But the final push is when Da Vinci opens the door and gives her "wings to fly" into the arms of her lover.

#18 R9 – The Lovers Reunite. Somehow they find a way to get together despite the huge obstacles. It may be brief, but this is the scene where they admit/realize they both are fated to love each other and profess that love. This is a fun scene because they still can't unite fully.

#19 R10 – Complications Push Them Apart. There is one last big obstacle in their way. Which sends them reeling into the high action and tension of . . .

#9 (also **#20 – R11** – Together at Last) Turning Point #5 (76-99%). The climax in which the goal is either reached or not; the two MDQs are answered.

#10 – The aftermath (90-99%). The wrap-up at the end. Denouement, resolution, tie it all in a pretty knot.

#20 R12 – The HEA. A final, parting shot of the happy result of the wrap-up. This could be included in the last scene (above) as the two plot elements merge together, or they might be separate scenes within the final chapter(s).

Note: R1 is essentially scene #1, R11 is scene #9, and R12 is scene #20. So you have basically the twenty key scenes here, give or take one or two depending on how you want to lay this out.

But note that once you have all this sketched in, you are way ahead of the game! The key, as I mentioned, is that subplot.

In my Westerns, I have bad guys going after gold, parents standing in the way of the lovers aching to unite, and even a grizzly bear acting as the opposition that brings the lovers together, tears them apart, then pulls them back united in a fight for their lives.

Wow, I know this is a lot to take in. But I hope you see how I built off those initial ten scenes and laid in the requisite romance scenes so that the romance story engine is in place. Now—you can get to work on the next ten to add in all the added excitement, stakes, and obstacles.

Yes, I made a chart that you can work with, and you can download it at Live Write Thrive. It gives you these twenty basic scenes and the 12 Key Romance scenes Michael Hauge recommends.

* * *

Your assignment: Print out the 12-Scene Romance Chart and start figuring out your twelve key romance scenes. If you've already laid out your first layer of ten scenes, see if you can layer in the romance ones in the right places. If you're not writing a romance, get working on your either your subplot layer or your action-reaction layer!

Chapter 13: The Romance Layer on Display

I've shown you one way you might integrate the key romance scenes into your foundational ten scenes.

Yes, it can be a daunting—but fun!—process to layer in your scenes. I hear some of you complaining.

But listen—writing a novel is hard. You can do it the really hard way or you can smooth out the path and make it way easier. The hard way is to wing it—go ahead and waste months of your life. I can write a novel in about a month if I plot it out carefully using this method. You can too.

If you are clear about your ten key scenes and have them in their approximate place, you've done the hard work of getting the big rocks in the jar. Those pebbles can fit into all the spaces between the rocks. You may have to jiggle the jar a bit to get them to settle in, but that's part of the process.

You've seen how romance novels have a very specific structure and story engine. That's another framework you can use to help you have solid structure for your story.

So now, I'm going to show you how useful this method is.

When I first wrote this section as a series of blog posts, I'd just started writing my fifth installment in my Front Range series—historical Western romance set in Colorado in the 1870s. When I began brainstorming this novel, I decided to go straight into using this method and started with my ten key scenes.

I first, of course, worked out my basic plot idea, my themes, key characters, opposition, and high stakes. The goal for the book is always clear in a romance novel—the girl wants to get the guy or vice versa despite obstacles and forces keeping them apart.

We looked at Michael Hauge's "Lover's Journey" list of key scenes, which I'll again utilize in this chapter.

Breakdown of *Colorado Dream*

Once I had all the basic components I needed, I began laying out those ten scenes.

The story in *Colorado Dream* centers on a heroine whose dream is to become a principal violinist in the NY Phil and a hero, a rough and tumble troubled cow-puncher, whose gift is breaking wild horses.

As is intrinsic to romance novels, the two are as different as can be, yet they are perfect for each other. They both land in Colorado— she's there to buy a violin from a master instrument maker in Greeley, and he arrives half-dead after being chased and shot at and running from trouble.

Like a wild horse, my hero is untamable, restless, unable to find peace due to heavy guilt hanging around his neck. Yet, when my heroine plays her violin, he is strangely calmed—similar to how horses respond to his voice. The more he fights her magical spell, the more entangled he becomes . . . and of course falls in love.

The horse whisperer meets the cowboy whisperer. Or something like that.

The Key to Success Lies in the Subplot

In order to have a strong story, I needed a strong subplot. For, in my opinion, the best romance novels are all about the subplot.

Remember: the main plot is the "guy meets girl, guy gets girl." In other words, the romance story is the main engine driving the story, which is what I explained in the previous chapter. But while that in itself may have interesting and original components due to the character types and background issues, what really makes a great romance read is a subplot that works to create the opposition, heighten the stakes, and prevent the lovers from getting together.

Strong subplots can be the source of misdirection, twists, complications, setbacks, and all sorts of great novel elements. (Hence . . . the practicality of using the Ten Key Scene Chart to ensure those conflict-packed scenes are figured in.)

So, I came up with a basic subplot that is set in motion before the novel starts. In fact, moments before the first scene with my hero Brett, he was at a cowboy competition (precursor to what we now know as a rodeo). As he was readying to leave, he saw a rich rancher's son trying to rape a woman. He interfered and a fight ensued, followed by the chase scene that is shown in his first scene.

What Brett doesn't know is that after he is shot in the leg, his return shots have hit his pursuer and caused the rich rancher-son-would-be-rapist to fall and smash on the ground, leaving him paralyzed. This sets off an enraged father whose goal is now to find Brett and make him pay—with his life.

A good subplot, as I showed in a previous chapter, will build just as the main plot builds, and at the climax of the novel will also build to a strong climax, and then will resolve either at the climax or shortly after.

Let's grab the 20-scene structure I shared with you in the last chapter. I'll plug in my story's scenes into this chart in boldface (remember the scenes marked with **R** are the layered romance scenes):

Breakdown of *Colorado Dream*'s 20 Key Scenes

#1 (also R1) – Setup. Introduce protagonist (heroine) in her world. Establish her core need. Set the stage, begin building the world. **New York: Angela tries to sneak off to the train station to leave for Greeley to get her violin. Mother tries to dissuade. Father chases after the train. Establish her father's violence and that her mother will no doubt suffer from helping Angela leave.**

#11 R1 –introduction of HERO. This is the match to the first essential scene. **Brett is being chased by three guys, gets shot at, hits the open range of CO, shoots back, gets lost in a dust storm, wanders the desert, has to shoot injured horse, dying of thirst in the heat.**

#2 Turning Point #1 (10%) Inciting Incident. This incident moves the heroine into position for the meet (a move to another location, an event, etc.). **Angela in Greeley at the violin-maker's house. Brett is next door recovering, after being found nearly dead by a local doctor. They are positioned to meet.**

#12 R2 – The Meet. **Brett hears her play violin at night. He's very moved, goes outside. They meet, but there is friction because he fights the attraction and power of her music. She finds him crass and uncouth.**

#3 Pinch Point #1 (33%). Give a glimpse of the opposition's power, need, and goal as well as the stakes. This is the full setup of your subplot, against which your lovers face conflict, opposition, and obstacles. **Introduction of subplot! We see the rich rancher, Orlander, angry that his son has been paralyzed. He sends his men out to search for Brett to kill him. He is lied to about what happened (important later).**

#13 R4 – Wise Friend Counsels. The hero and heroine can each have a mentor/ally/wise friend character that gives them advice regarding their love life and/or pushing them to consider the potential love interest. **Both hero and heroine have a "wise counselor." The doctor helping Brett recover helps land Brett a job at big rancher Logan's cattle company outside of town. Angela finds a mentor in the kind violin-maker (recently widowed)—the father she wished she had.**

#4 Twist #1. Something new happens: a new ally, a friend becomes a foe. New info reveals a serious complication to reaching the goal. **Brett gets the job at the ranch, but a top (arrogant) ranch hand is humiliated by him and ends up losing his job. Sets up antagonist that will align with Orlander's men to attack Brett at the climax. Angela gets a job at the same ranch to teach violin to Logan's young daughters. This twist brings them together but also creates problems. Set up allies for Brett—cowboys at the ranch he helps and encourages. Angela learns her mother hospitalized by her father dragging her from the train platform. She is grieved, and Fisk (violin-**

maker) consoles her and encourages her to stay a while and not rush home to her angry father.

#14 R5 – Acknowledge Interest. A key scene that throws the lovers together so they start getting to really know each other. **A first scene of the two lovers spending time together on the ranch. She sees his gift in taming horses. They learn a bit about each other and note that they both have violent fathers. She sees he is hiding something (his guilt over his mother's death at his father's hand—same situation as hers, in essence). Note: it's so important to have some key early scenes in which the two lovers start getting to know each other. Too many writers rush their characters into love, which is unbelievable. They have to see in what ways they are alike.**

#5 The Midpoint (50%). No turning back. Important event that propels the story forward and solidifies the protagonist's determination to reach her goal. Usually one of the lovers realizes and decides the other is for them, and they will now pursue without letup, despite current obstacles. And at the same time, the other may see something that makes him/her decide the relationship is not gonna happen. **Brett convinces Angela to go for a ride with him. She's never ridden before. When they land in a nest of rattlesnakes, Brett goes crazy in killing them. She is afraid of his violent streak (as is he, which is his big fear—that he'll end up like his violent father). She decides it's time to go back to NY. The West is too wild and scary. Brett is falling for her but doesn't know how to win her heart.**

#15 R6 – The First Quarrel. Things start coming to a head and creating high tension with the lovers. **Brett hears/sees she is leaving and tries to stop her. She promises the rancher's wife she won't leave until after she performs her violin at the big birthday party for the rancher. Their differences seem too great to reconcile.**

#6 Pinch Point #2 (62%). The opposition comes full force. Time to buckle down and fight through it. Again, this is further *development of the subplot*. The nemesis or opposition is going to make it nearly impossible for the couple to get together. **Fight at the roundup. Brett angers two of Logan's hands. They quit and storm off. Connect with Orlander's men, who've arrived in town, following leads to Brett. They team up and plot killing Brett at the big birthday bash at the ranch (climax situation).**

#16 R7 – The Dance of Attraction. The two are again thrown together, and now they are perilously close to falling madly in love. But . . . there are still obstacles (subplot unresolved) and emotional resistance due to fear and doubt and past wounds. **Big firestorm across the prairie. Brett and hands are taking horses to the park for a cowboy event. He helps to save picnickers and Angela and gets them to safety. She sees how self-sacrificing he is in saving others. Not what she expected. His almost losing her makes him realizes how smitten he is.**

#7 Twist 2. An unexpected surprise giving (false?) hope. The goal now looks within reach. A mentor gives encouragement, a secret weapon, or an important clue. Events occur to make this romance look possible, giving hope. **Angela gets position with the opera, with Fisk's help. She thinks about staying and making her life here. Brett hears she's staying.**

#17 R8 – The Black Moment. Then something happens to kill the possibility of a true romance. A misdirection, lie, reversal, misunderstanding. **Angela mishears and misunderstands someone, thinking Brett killed someone and is a wanted man. She thinks he's lied to her. Rejects him. He doesn't know why.**

#8 Turning Point #4 (75%). Major setback. All is lost and hopeless. Time for final push. **Brett seeks her out and tells her the truth, begs her to believe him. She is conflicted.**

#18 R9 – The Lovers Reunite. Somehow they find a way to get together despite the huge obstacles. This is the scene where they admit/realize they both are fated to love each other and profess that love. **They are at the ranch party. He hears her play the violin and this time lets it reach his heart and wound, which scares him. But now he knows he is in love. They talk, he** shares his wound, she realizes she loves him. But their worlds are still apart.

#19 R10 – Complications Push Them Apart. There is one last big obstacle in their way. Which sends them reeling into the high action and tension of the Climax. **Big fight and shooting scene at the ranch. Orlander is caught, and rancher and Brett are brought before Logan to face off. The truth all comes out.**

#9 (also #20 – R11 – Together at Last) Turning Point #5 (76-99%). The climax in which the goal is either reached or not; the two MDQs are answered. **Brett is exonerated. Angela sees he is innocent and a hero, not a villain.**

#10 The aftermath (90-99%). The wrap-up at the end. Denouement, resolution, tie it all in a pretty knot. **Angela makes her decision to stay in Greeley and teach music and play with the local opera orchestra. Brett, no longer running, becomes Logan's foreman of the ranch. The lovers can now be together.**

#20 R12 – The HEA. A final, parting shot of the happy result of the wrap-up. **A happy Christmas party that brings all the players on stage. Brett receives money as compensation from the rich rancher, so he can now marry Angela and buy property to start a horse ranch (his dream).**

Some of these scenes got moved around as I wrote, but laying out these scenes gave me a foundation to work with. From this, I created a whole lot of other scenes to connect the existing ones—the sand that gets poured into the jar and fills in around the pebbles. Those scenes involve action with secondary characters who serve as key allies to both characters.

The novel is now finished and was a lot of fun to write. Using the chart made it easy!

Remember, there are many ways to vary this, but I hope this look at my process with a recent novel—using this structure I'm sharing with you—is giving you lots of ideas. Use the charts; they were created to help you!

And if you aren't sure yet what those ten key scenes should be, study *The 12 Key Pillars of Novel Construction* and use the workbook! If you work through all the brainstorming questions and checklists, you'll get to that solid story.

Seriously, too many writers suffer fear and loathing when it comes to writing a novel. You don't have to. With a bit of work and planning, you can take the pain out, and guess what's left? The fun!

I love writing novels. I'm on my twenty-first (I think). I want you to love writing novels too! And I believe you will if you use this layering method.

* * *

Your assignment: If you're writing a romance, plot out your second layer of romance scenes over your key ten scenes. Take some time to thumb through your favorite romance novels and find first the ten key scenes, then the ten romance scenes that make up the second layer.

If you don't write romance, you get a pass!

Chapter 14: What about the Next Layer?

We've nailed the first layer: the ten key scenes. That's the strong foundation for just about any story. That next layer? You've seen how you could come up with a solid and relevant subplot and layer those scenes in among the first ten. You've also seen how you might focus on action-reaction to craft those next ten scenes. And if you're writing in the romance genre, you now have a handy method to layering in romance scenes in a way that befits the genre.

But twenty scenes does not a full-length novel make. So we're going talk a bit about the third layer: scenes 21-30. This layer is really all about pouring the sand into your jar to fill all the remaining spaces (though, granted, you may have many more than thirty total scenes).

Every layer builds on the previous layer. At some point you are going to be done with your layers. How do you know when to stop layering?

Good question. We don't want cakes with fifty layers that topple over or collapse under the weight of the icing. And with our "Is it full yet?" jar of rocks, we don't have a jar that reaches heaven. It has to be a practical size to be functional. And so does a novel.

Here's how I look at it.

Every scene must serve a purpose in your story. If you have a scene that doesn't advance your plot in a meaningful way or reveal something important about the characters, or both, it shouldn't be in your novel.

That's the first test of a scene. And it's a big one.

Thirty scenes might be just the right number (give or take a few) for a novella. Some novels may have around thirty scenes—we saw *Catching Fire* with about twenty-seven chapters. I don't know what the word count is for that novel; the hardcover edition has 390 pages, but the font is large and set with wide line spacing and big margins (which is done to help a short book look long), so it seems more like a novella than a typical novel at about 80,000 words.

I like to quote (or paraphrase, since I can't remember the exact words) Donald Maass, who, when asked at his weeklong workshop how long a novel should be, answered, "As long as it needs to be."

Novellas and Their Key Scenes

A novella isn't going to have the depth a novel should have. You may not have any subplots. The story may take place over a mere few days rather than months.

My historical Western romance novella *Wild Secret, Wild Longing* lands fairly long at about 47,000 words and takes place over about four days all told. A lot of action and character development takes place in that short amount of time, and it's a challenge to write a rich and believable story in so few words. This installment in my series has fourteen chapters that comprise about eighteen or so scenes.

This novella has no subplot. If it did, it would have become a novel. My objective, however, was to write a short and sweet (though intense) story of how LeRoy Banks falls in love.

So, the scope of your plot and the demands of your premise will dictate, for the most part, whether you'll be writing a novella or a novel. But focus on making the story "as long as it needs to be." And deconstruct best-selling works in your niche genre so you can make sure your book will fit right in alongside them—in both length and structure.

I'm going to summarize the chapters in *Wild Secret, Wild Longing* so you can see how this story, even though a short one, uses the ten-key scene structure, and the romance structure as well. (Note: this summary contains spoilers here, in case you're thinking you'd like to read this book.) I've put in bold the key scenes. Even though this is an unusual plot, I made sure to lock in those foundational scenes and build from there.

Some of the key scenes are missing, such as "Wise Friends Counsels" (it's just the hero and heroine trapped alone in a cabin), but you can still see how the framework is supported by most of those foundational scenes in the right places.

Wild Secret, Wild Longing

Chapter 1: **#1 (and #R1) and #2 – The Setup and the Inciting Incident**. LeRoy (hero) is at his brother Eli's wedding and feeling a bit lonely. His mother hints that maybe it's time he found a wife and, as per her usual mysteriousness, warns that the mountains hold secrets. Will his heart be ready? The Inciting Incident barrels in near the end of this chapter: a grizzly attacks the horses at this ranch where LeRoy's employed. The beast is shot and dangerous, and someone must hunt it down and kill it. LeRoy is the best tracker, so he knows it's up to him.

Chapter 2: **#11 R1 – Introduction of the Heroine.** We meet Genevieve (heroine), a woman living alone up the mountain. She is running out of supplies and can't bear the thought of trying to survive yet another lonely winter. But she has no other choice. She hears a wolf howling and knows danger is waiting outside her cabin. She grabs her rifle and heads out, with the first big winter storm approaching.

Chapter 3: LeRoy gets ready to head out after the bear. Other ranch hands prepare to chase it down too, but LeRoy goes alone, knowing those useless men won't find the bear. With a scene break, we watch Gennie head through the woods and realize that grizzly she'd seen before is back. She has to kill it before it kills her or her mule.

Chapter 4: **#12 R2 – The Meet (Yes, it is! Read on).** LeRoy tracks for hours, smells the smoke of a nearby cabin, then runs headlong into a massive growling wolf. Just as he's about to reluctantly shoot, something smashes him upside the head. When he comes to, he sees the man who struck him, and the wolf seems to be his pet. Turns out the man, Dan, is also hunting the grizzly. The unfriendly man allows LeRoy to join him.

Chapter 5: **Complication.** The two encounter the bear. LeRoy saves Dan's life by diverting the bear from attacking the fella. But then the bear attacks LeRoy, slicing open his stomach. Dan bandages him, then helps him get up and moving, and as snow falls, the wolf leads them to a cabin.

Chapter 6: #3 First Pinch Point. (To Gennie, LeRoy is the opposition she must best.) Gennie is inside her cabin, cursing over not finding that bear. Here we learn she is "Dan"—a woman pretending to be a man in order to survive in her world. She drags the injured half-breed into her cabin and tends to him, determined that he not find out her secret. She hates Indians because they had murdered her family and raped her when she was young, but this man saved her life, and he's handsome, to boot. His presence generates huge inner conflict. She wants to get him healed and out of her cabin ASAP.

Chapter 7: #4 Twist #1. Next morning LeRoy wakes, goes outside with the wolf and makes friends with it. "Dan" gives him breakfast and warns him not to snoop, then heads out to do chores. LeRoy doesn't know what to make of his host. Outside, Gennie despairs at the already heavy snowfall, knowing she won't last another winter. Then her mule brays, and she sees the grizzly going after it. This is the last straw. She will die trying to kill that grizzly. She fires her gun. Inside the cabin, LeRoy hears the shot, and though hardly able to walk, heads out, tracking her steps in the deep snow. A snow-heavy branch crashes on Gennie and knocks her out. LeRoy rushes to her aid. He shoots and kills the bear, then finds "Dan" almost dead and lugs the "fella" back to the cabin. (These are via multiple scene breaks and POV shifts.)

Chapter 8: #5 The Midpoint – no turning back. Back in the cabin, LeRoy tends to unconscious "Dan." Very quickly he realizes Dan is a woman. LeRoy ponders her situation, dire indeed. Gennie comes to, and LeRoy assures her the bear is dead, not letting on he knows her secret. The snow has them trapped inside, and LeRoy learns more about this amazingly brave woman. His strong feelings for her now cannot be ignored.

Chapter 9: #6 Pinch Point #2 (Gennie feels exposed by her "opposition") While LeRoy naps, Gennie thinks about her lonely life, then starts to cry. LeRoy awakes, and from his expression, she knows he knows her secret. She feels exposed and trapped, so she flees, wanting to die.

(No #7 twist here, but twists were added before the Midpoint)

#8 Dark Night moment for LeRoy. LeRoy, still hobbling takes off after her in the heavy snow, with her wolf leading him. He nearly dies in the blizzard but presses on and finds her half dead. It takes him forever, but he manages to get her back to the cabin alive.

Chapter 10: **#15 R6 – The First Quarrel.** Gennie wakes, they have the "big" talk in which they share their hearts and fears and begin to see how they are alike in many ways, but there is resistance. LeRoy has already fallen in love with her. He pries out her story and learns what happened to her and why she is hiding in the mountains. Gennie believes she is tainted and has no place in the real world down the mountain. LeRoy shares his heart and tells her she has value and to stop blaming herself. They kiss.

Chapter 11: **#9 The hero reaches his goal (getting the girl).** Next morning, LeRoy ponders what to do and how he might convince Gennie to leave with him once the storm passes. He knows she's terrified at the thought of joining humanity. Gennie wakes, aware that she is falling for LeRoy. Over breakfast he tells her his plan. She resists but decides to trust him. He's saved her life twice. But he assures her she's saved his as well.

Chapter 12: **#18 R9 – The lovers are united.** A few days later they are headed down the hill on his horse, mule and wolf following.

#19 R10 – One last big obstacle. They run into the two lost ranch hands, who make lewd advances on Gennie. LeRoy punches them, putting them in their place and showing Gennie he meant what he said about protecting her. It also helps that her wolf is a frightening sight. LeRoy takes their horses and makes them walk down the mountain.

Chapter 13: **#20 R11 – Together at last. They've made it (She reaches her goal here—to rejoin society).** Gennie gets nervous as they approach the ranch and everyone welcomes them back. She learns quickly that all those scary people are actually kind and loving. The women take her off to bathe her and give her beautiful clothes. A Cinderella moment.

Chapter 14: **#10 and #20 R12 – The wrap-up and the HEA.** LeRoy, at dinner and waiting for Gennie, talks to his ma, who's worked it all out. Gennie will go to their ranch with his ma and the wolf, and LeRoy will finish up his time at this ranch, keeping his promise to help break the wild horses he and his brother had caught (prior novel's plot). LeRoy is besotted by Gennie's transformation, and they share a kiss full of promise and joy.

I hope you can see from this elaborate breakdown how you can plot out a novel or novella of any reasonable length and make this general structure work. If you feel a novel is too daunting a starting place, consider plotting out a novella with those first two layers. If you're not doing a romance, try the action-reaction method (since it's hard to develop a strong subplot in so few pages, though I'm sure it could be done).

Don't Neglect Scene Structure

Aim for purpose and economy of scenes. Every scene must serve a purpose. And now that you understand novel framework, it's not all that hard!

I hope you noticed in my breakdown of my novella that every scene contained important action, inner and/or outer conflict, and story advancement. You don't see characters sitting around merely talking about the weather and deciding what to eat for dinner.

Let me just add this for good measure: to make this layering method work, you also need to nail scene structure. Scenes are like mini novels. They should start in the middle of something happening, build to a climax, reveal something important (the high moment), then end (resolve or hang).

Approach building a scene the same way you tackle building a novel. And if you need help on scene structure, I have more charts that can help you! Hop over to my blog Live Write Thrive and grab them from my resource page.

Once you have those twenty scenes in place, you may only need a few more, as I did in *Wild Secret, Wild Longing,* to fill up the jar.

But if you're aiming for a novel, you'll need at least a third layer. Let's take a look at one example, building on what we've looked at in previous chapters.

The Third Layer Using the Subplot Method

A few chapters back, I shared my twenty layered scenes from my detective novel *A Thin Film of Lies*. In this chapter, I'll show you how I added in ten more scenes (sand) over the twenty previously laid out (rocks and pebbles). I used the subplot method, but when you work on the third layer, the objective is the same for whichever method you use. Think: *connecting*.

What you need to do at this point in your layering is focus on smooth transitioning between scenes. If you have a twist, then a reaction scene, then the Midpoint, you might notice you're missing a scene that helps segue from reaction to Midpoint. If you've had a lot of high-action scenes in a row, it may be time for a low-energy reflection scene. With any of these methods, it helps to identify which scenes are high energy and which are low (you can color-code them on your chart) to see where you could use more action, reaction, processing, or decision scenes.

Here is the chart once more for *A Thin Film of Lies*. The first ten scenes are the foundational scenes, inserted in the right places in the framework. The next ten pertain to the subplot. And while you don't need exactly ten subplot scenes, again, this is just done to give a simple template or method. Veer as you wish, but make it work best for the story you are telling.

I've noted in bold this third layer—the additional ten scenes I'm adding in. Take a look at how these scenes bridge the bigger ones—essentially filling in those spaces.

What purpose do those additional scenes have? Some show the reaction to the previous action. Some show the processing that follows a reaction. Others show the decision that follows the processing, initiating a new action.

In other words, you need to be keenly aware of the natural action-reaction-process-decision cycle. Your characters should act naturally, and sometimes this process all takes place in only a part of a scene; other times this process covers many scenes. And those are often the "filler" scenes.

Make sense?

Once you get this nailed, you should be able to grab any great novel and chart it out. You should find that these key scenes are in just the right places and with these "connecting" scenes between them.

So here's my chart (and remember, the numbering relates to the layering, but the scenes are laid out in order *as the story unfolds*). This may look daunting and complex, but what follows is almost the entire novel plotted out, which translates to more than 100,000 words. So it should be fairly complex.

Instead of being intimidated by the breadth and scope of layering, try to view this as your roadmap to success.

A Thin Film of Lies Subplot Layer

#1 Setup. Introduce protagonist in her world. Establish her core need. After prologue setting up Libby's death, we meet Fran Anders, homicide detective, called to the scene of the hit-and-run. She gets an anonymous call while there stating this was murder.

#21 **Meet Alisa, the wife of the suspected murderer. Begin subplot of her character. Set up tension in marriage, letters she gets from "Libby" before she's killed.**

#11 Introduction of subplot. Set up the situation between the characters to show the existing tension and attitudes that is causing conflict. Fran is concerned about her son's behavior. They are disconnected, and the tenth anniversary of her husband's disappearance is approaching. He's having problems with kids at school.

#2 Turning Point #1 (10%). Inciting Incident. Fran meets Mike Jepson—he's the suspect, and she now starts investigating him. He claims he's innocent.

#22 **More development in the investigation. Mike and Alisa have been interrogated. Alisa claims she caused the dent in the car. Fran wants Ident to check out the bumper. (New action that leads to processing, decision, and new action.)**

#12 Show how the Inciting Incident affects the subplot. It may trigger it, bring it to the forefront. Have something initially happen with the subplot to bring in problems and complications. Fran goes as chaperone on a class trip with son. At the park, she stumbles upon a drug sale gone violent that involves a couple of Trevor's classmates and intervenes. Trevor is angry and embarrassed at her mother's cop actions.

#3   Pinch Point #1 (33% roughly). Give a glimpse of the opposition's power, need, and goal as well as the stakes. Alisa secretly meets with Mike's best friend, finds out Mike had had an affair years ago. Trust erodes. Alisa decides to investigate Mike's claim he was at the club nights. (Her husband, essentially, becomes the opposition to her.)

#23 Fran questions an acquaintance of the deceased and learns key info that advances the investigation. (New action, followed by processing.)

#13   New subplot development that mirrors or is opposite of the main plot. In other words, show what key opposition your protagonist is facing and how she feels about it. Fran is called in to school. Trevor is in the principal's office, accused of hacking the school's computers to change grades. He swears he's innocent but evidence proves otherwise. Parallels Fran's case, with Jepson arrested for hit-and-run and swearing he's innocent.

#4   Twist #1. Something new happens: a new ally, a friend becomes a foe. New info reveals a serious complication to reaching the goal. Protagonist must adjust to change with this setback. This twist pertains to the main plot. Mike finds items planted in his car from Libby. He's starting to lose it. Alisa now doesn't believe his innocence anymore (perfect example of "friend becomes a foe"). Cops come and check out the dent in the car.

#24 Alisa leaves to stay in a hotel. Mike begs his friend to help him. Things look bleak for Mike. (New action, followed by reaction and processing.)

#14   Progress with the subplot. Similar to the main plot, the character is trying to deal with the subplot issues, complications, and setbacks. Tension builds as things are getting more difficult or problematic. Fran plays softball with coworkers. Reveals the backstory about her marriage, her husband leaving without a word ten years ago, that ten-year anniversary looming, and how it ties in with her disconnect with Trevor, how she's tried to be the best mom but feels she's failed.

#25   A mother at the day care where Alisa works (DeeDee) suddenly becomes her BFF and takes her to lunch. (Subtle but big development in the plot.)

#5   The Midpoint (50%). No turning back. Important event that propels the story forward and solidifies the protagonist's determination to reach her goal. Fran has to arrest Mike. She doesn't know if he's guilty, but she has no choice. Mike hires a PI from jail to help him. His life and marriage is in ruins. (Here it's a Midpoint moment for both the protagonist and the main secondary characters, Mike and Alisa.)

#15   Things start coming to a head and creating high tension with the subplot. Now that the protagonist is committed to going all-in after her goal, the subplot adds stress to her load. Fran is home. Daughter Megan arrives distraught. Her boyfriend broke up with her, feels she's unlovable. This unleashes Fran's insecurities and loneliness, and emphasizes Fran's need to be perfect and please everyone, never make a mistake.

#6   Pinch Point #2 (62% roughly). The opposition comes full force. Time to buckle down and fight through it. Mike meets with a lawyer who tells him there's no hope. Mike swears he's innocent. Falls apart. Deedee (who is the nemesis in the story) worms her way into Alisa's home and life and starts drugging her and manipulating her while Mike is in jail.

#26   Mike's lawyer pressures Mike to get through to Alisa. The lawyer is not on his side and paints a bleak picture. Alisa is falling hard under Deedee's manipulation. (New action creating huge complications, barreling toward the climax.)

#16   Developments with the subplot reach critical mass. Things are falling apart, looking hopeless. Fran doesn't believe her son is innocent—all evidence proves he hacked into the school's computer. Their relationship is threatened to break.

#7   Twist 2. An unexpected surprise giving (false?) hope. The goal now looks within reach. A mentor gives encouragement, a secret weapon, or an important clue. The PI Mike's hired finds clues to who is framing him. He has a name and now all evidence is showing she is the culprit (hope!). But she can't be found.

#27   Alisa works up courage to meet with Fran and talk. Fran gets her to turn back to God, and this moves Alisa to give Mike a chance to explain, and hence become his support once again. (Decision, which prompts new actions.)

#17   Subplot feels at a standstill. Protagonist has no time to deal with it and so this creates more tension. Or something in the subplot could provide the help, insight, clue the protagonist needs to push harder to the goal. Fran can't get through to Trevor, and she has no time to deal with him.

#27   Alisa visits Mike, she now believes in his innocence. PI is trying to find DeeDee. (Connecting scene for the main plot.)

#8   Turning Point #4 (75%). Major setback. All is lost and hopeless. Time for final push. The identity of Mike's nemesis is clear, but she can't be found. His arraignment is coming up. He dumps the bad lawyer and gets a new one. All looks hopeless.

#18   Same issues with the subplot. Seems unresolvable. Something happens that closes doors. Or the subplot might be resolved outwardly, but the desired emotional state is illusive. Fran finds Trevor at the park. She has good news—turns out, due to her efforts, that evidence proves Trevor was set up (just like Jepson). He gets angry—she didn't believe he was innocent even though he insisted he was. She mentions that his dad leaving is at the heart of all his pain. He feels like he's a loser and confesses that he believes that's why Dad left. Then he storms off. This starts Fran's descent into emotional darkness.

#28   Alisa, shocked, discovers her house guest is Mike's nemesis. Deedee attacks Alisa and leaves her for dead, heading to the arraignment. (Big complication.)

#9   Turning Point #5 (76-99%). The climax in which the goal is either reached or not; the two MDQs are answered. Mike is exonerated in court when evidence proves he didn't kill Libby. Deedee shows up in the courtroom about to mess with Mike further. The main plot goal (Mike trying to prove he is innocent) is resolved, but then . . .

#29   Mike ends up killing Deedee in the courthouse parking lot, then is taken into custody. Big twist at the end that puts him back in jail. (Adding a twist after the "supposed" climax is a great structural element.)

#19   The key scene that resolves the subplot in a completely satisfying, full way. The character has achieved the emotional resolution she's wanted from the start. After the main plot climax, Fran leaves the new crime scene and arrives home with blood on her clothes. Trevor freaks at the sight, and Fran is feeling completely vulnerable. Fran and Trevor have the healing heart-to-heart when Fran breaks down, blames herself for hubby leaving, for being a terrible mom, and realizes she's tried to be the perfect mom and that her efforts have backfired. She "comes into her essence" and the spiritual MDQ is resolved.

#10   The aftermath (90-99%). The wrap-up at the end. The wrap-up of the case for Fran. She's helped Mike, so he won't be in jail long. And she's helped Alisa return to God. For Fran, it's all wrapped up.

#30   Alisa accepts the outcome. Her character arc comes to completion. Mike has changed, and there is hope now for their marriage. Loose ends are tied up actually and emotionally. (Final processing scene.)

#20   A final, parting shot of the happy result of the subplot wrapped up. This could be included in the last scene (above) as the two plot elements merge together, or they might be separate scenes within the final chapter(s). **Three months later Mike is out of jail. But the case is resolved, and Alisa and Mike reunite and heal. Just as Fran and Trevor have healed their relationship.**

While there are more scenes in my novel, I hope you can see how this next layer brings in the additional scenes that advance the main plot, complicate, and resolve. Some of the scenes are processing. Some are ones in which characters make new decisions. Some are new actions based on those decisions.

So, study well the action-reaction cycle. Read great novels that portray characters exhibiting this natural behavior. This will go far in helping you create the scenes that will work as the sand that fills in the spaces between the pebbles.

While this may seem crazy and complicated, it really isn't. If you start with those ten key scenes and layer in the next ten most important scenes and the next, you will keep adding on to a strong framework. And a solidly built structure won't easily collapse.

* * *

Your assignment: Break down your favorite novel or one you just read. As you skim through the book, jot down the summary of each scene—maybe one or two sentences. Then, once you have all the scenes written down, try to identify first the ten key scenes, then the second set of scenes, followed by the third layer of scenes.

Note what types of scenes are used to bridge the key scenes. Pay attention to which scenes are action, reaction, processing, or new action. I'll bet you you'll learn a lot by doing this.

Part 3: Layers in Contemporary Best-Selling Novels

Chapter 15: What Analysis Can Teach You

In these next chapters, I'm going to summarize a few novels I've recently read—best sellers in different genres—and do what I did with *Catching Fire*. I want you to see how these ten key scenes are typical of well-structured novels, regardless of whether the author had any forethought about such a method.

I'm also going to share with you a couple of titles that, while being best sellers, to me fail the test. The structure is flawed, and, as I reader, I found these novels losing my interest midway through. In fact, I had to press through to finish them for the sake of my analysis.

When I set out to read a novel that sounds intriguing, I'm always looking for that brilliant story. We search for those gems in the dirt—the rare novels that grab us and don't let us go until the end. And those are the types of novels we authors want to write.

I'm so often disappointed. I wonder if you are too. Sometimes the writing is mediocre and boring. The characters are flat or unlikable or stereotyped. There are a lot of reasons a novel might fail our personal test of "brilliant." And usually, to me, the biggest problem lies in the structure.

C. S. Lakin

There Are a Lot of Lousy Novels Out There

There are a lot of best sellers out there that are pretty lousy stories. Some are just plain boring. Some are written badly. Some are horribly structured. Just because a novel has hit the top of the *New York Times* Bestseller List, it doesn't mean it's a great book.

I hope you don't think I'm being arrogant. I apologize if I come across this way. Over the years I've groused with fellow authors about this sorry state of book publishing. We want to tear our hair out when we read some of these "masterpieces."

However, a lot of people like these novels and sing their praises. What can I say? As you read through, maybe even deconstruct, some of those "great" novels in your mission to understand strong novel structure, you may end up scratching your head.

All this to say: I hope once you have solid novel structure deeply ingrained in your brain, you'll be quick to spot where novels fail. Where their weak sections are and why. How you might have structured that novel differently to make it work—regardless of whether they have "Bestseller" written on the cover.

I also hope you will see, in time, over the long term, that starting with those ten key scenes in the right places is most often the best decision. And that you'll adopt this layering method as *your* go-to method for success.

Intuitive Layering

I recently chatted with a close friend who is an award-winning novelist and a "sworn pantser," something we joke about, as she ribs me about being so overly organized, and I chide her for winging it and suffering the accompanying agony. All kidding aside, when she asked me about this book I've been writing and I described my layering method, her reaction was one of surprise. "Hey, that's what I do," she said. "I start with a handful of key scenes, then I add in the transitional scenes . . ."

So, though she would never say she is a plotter, she is surely a "layerer," and I hope that, if you're a sworn pantser too, you'll give this layering approach more than a cursory consideration.

But as you've seen, there is more to this method than coming up with ten important scenes in your novel and just sticking them where they "feel right." My author friend may intuitively, after writing so

138

many great novels, place those key scenes in just the right spots. Stephen King brags how he never plots, but I would bet you the farm (if I had one) that he has this structure so ingrained in him that those key scenes are usually right where they're supposed to be.

Yes, these analyses are a lot to take in. A lot to read.

I hesitated when considering doing these extensive novel summaries, not because they take a lot of time on my part but because they require a lot of reading on your part. But my desire to have you truly *get* that strong novel framework is critical won out. By taking a hard look at novel scene outlines and identifying the structure, across multiple genres, you should be able to see the big picture of story structure. I hope you will take the time to go through all these analyses and master this layering concept.

No, Genre Doesn't Matter

And I also hope you'll see how this method works across genres.

Granted, a lot of novels veer off traditional structure and still work. With mainstream genres like thrillers and cozy mysteries, you may not see much sidetracking. But with other genres, such as contemporary and literary fiction, it may be more common. As with anything, some people break all the rules and they still succeed. But that's a risky endeavor. Often the authors who veer off track are those with millions of faithful followers who either readily or reluctantly trail along. I wouldn't recommend it for an aspiring writer.

You may find, as you deconstruct novels and start plotting out your scenes, that the layering method in this book doesn't fit your purposes. And that's fine. However, I would urge you, especially if you are new to novel writing, to try this first. Try coloring inside the lines before grabbing a paintbrush and sliding off the page and onto the dining table.

Feel free to experiment and play around with structure. But if your story feels stuck or begins wandering off into the hinterlands, rein it back in and work on those ten foundational scenes. See if you can't at least make your story work within that basic structure.

Novels That Just Don't Fit the Framework

Often novels are relational dramas—all about the characters and how they change, with little plot to speak of. And there is a place in the world of readers for these types of stories, many of which are wonderful beyond words.

So if you find that when you deconstruct *well-written* novels in your niche genre and summarize their scenes you can't come up with the obvious ten key scenes, that doesn't mean this method of layering doesn't apply. I'll venture to say that, with a bit of scrutiny, you will still find the basic story structure underlying the plot. There will still be those markers or milestones along the way that serve as foundational scenes—scenes that support the story as framework. And this is what we're focusing on here when we talk about layering.

If you can identify the important moments in the plot—when characters change, when events create a definitive shift in opinion, thinking, belief—those are the scenes to look for.

A Look at Contemporary YA

Contemporary Young Adult novels often fall into this category. You might find a story made up of diary entries—a high school girl telling what happens during the school year. Or you might come across a novel about teens struggling in a "coming of age" story. When you have a novel in which not a whole lot of "plot" is going on, if it's a terrific story, you should be able to see a clear and deliberate structure hidden below the surface of character exploration.

Let's take a good, long look at a recent best seller in the YA Contemporary genre. I found this novel by searching Amazon best sellers and bought a copy. This novel is a perfect example of a "coming of age" character-driven story with little plot.

The Serpent King by Jeff Zentner is set in rural Tennessee and alternates POV between three high school seniors who are misfits and struggling with their identity. Basically, this is a novel showing how Dill, Lydia, and Travis move from their persona to their true essence. In other words, by the end of the novel they grow, mature, face who they "really are," and finally accept and like themselves.

It's a hard, painful journey, and the "point" of the novel is succinctly expressed by the author: "I wanted to write about young people who struggle to lead lives of dignity and find beauty in a forgotten, unglamorous place."

In my opinion, novels with little plot are highly dependent on great characters, clever and engaging dialogue, and deep inner conflict to be successful. *The Serpent King* delivers on all these counts.

As I lay out the scene summary and identify what I believe are the ten key scenes, pay attention to how these moments in the story create a strong first layer to build upon.

Again, I have no way of knowing how this author or any other authors plot out novels, but that's beside the point. If a novel shows a clear, strong framework, to me, that's the main reason for its success. It needs those ten key scenes in the right places.

You might write your scenes out of order or without considering order or placement. But if, at some point, you step back and examine where in your novel these important scenes are located and you don't have a good sense of structure, your framework might collapse. You need to be able to move scenes around, or add or delete scenes, to get that framework strong. Using this layering method will help you move your pieces into place for maximum support of your story.

So, let's look at the fifty-three scenes (some are half a page) of *The Serpent King*.

With all these novel breakdowns, there are going to be spoilers, and there's a huge one in this book. So, while I apologize for the spoilers, they are necessary. If you want to read these novels first, put this book down and grab and read them. Then jump back in and study the breakdown.

Summary of *The Serpent King*

Let me give you a brief summary of this novel. Dillard Wayne Early Junior is the son of a charismatic preacher who is serving time in prison for child pornography. Dill is in a pitiable situation because he not only lives in a small town in which everyone knows what's happened with his father, his parents (and many congregants) also blame Dill for Dad's demise. His parents are fanatically religious and highly hypocritical. Instead of lying under oath and claiming the porn was his (since, being a minor, he wouldn't have gone to jail), Dill told the truth, and Dad was carted off. His parents are furious at him, and his mom piles on the guilt as she works exhausting hours trying to support Dill and herself, living in total denial and blaming him.

Dill, in all his misery, is infatuated with Lydia, a girl who has a funny dentist father and supportive mother, who provide her with a wonderful home life—in sharp contrast to Dill's pathetic home situation.

All Lydia wants is for senior year to hurry up so she can leave for New York and college. She's snarky, bossy, sophisticated, and, as a result, a misfit in this close-minded backwater town. She is somewhat famous, having carved out a niche online with her fashion blog. She is as ambitious as Dill is not. While she hangs out with Dill and enjoys his friendship, she's domineering and pushy, albeit with a snappy wit and measurable affection.

And then we have Travis. If Dill's home life is bad, Travis's is downright awful. His brother died fighting in Afghanistan, his drunk father beats and humiliates him (and terrifies him), and his weak mother does nothing to prop Travis up. He immerses himself in online sites all centered on a fantasy book series called Bloodfall. There he chats with others and gets into character, though this escape from his painful reality only partially provides relief. Lydia and Dill hang with Travis—an unlikely threesome, but misfits tend to gravitate together.

And so the story begins.

I've put in bold what I believe are the ten key scenes. I hope you'll see that, while they are not big plot events, they are big, *consequential* moments in which the characters are faced with choices and potential change. I hope you can see that even a novel that seems to ignore time-tested structure in fact may comply.

I know this is a lot of material, but I believe that by examining the scene breakdowns of novels in your genre, identifying the ten key scenes, then the next layer of ten scenes, you'll get the hang of this layering method—and you'll see how logical it is to plot out your story this way. (The POV character is named at the start of each scene summary.)

The Serpent King Scene Summary

1. **Key Scene #1 – Setup.** Dill: It's the day before school starts. He's playing guitar and thinking about Lydia. Establishes his talent and that his mother works at a motel. Lydia is about to pick Dill up to take him clothes shopping in Nashville for school. Mom pressures Dill to go visit Dad in prison while there. He doesn't want to go but can't say no. We meet Lydia and see how pushy and snarky she is as they pick up Travis, who carts his wizard staff with him wherever he goes. Scene ends with Dill feeling dread over the school year.

2. Lydia: The three go into a store in Nashville. She picks clothes for Dill, but Travis doesn't want any. She dickers with the shop owner to give them a deal, revealing Lydia is the famous blogger of Dollywould, a top fashion blog. This scene is all about setting up who Lydia is, her sophistication, her drive to be more, her need to go off to college and ditch this town.

3. Dill: Lydia and Travis wait at the prison while Dill goes in to visit his crazy dad. Dad preaches at him, as usual, pressuring him to sing and play guitar for Jesus. A total downer. Lydia takes him home and gives him a music CD to listen to. He is miserable.

4. Travis: After he's dropped off at home, we meet his horrible drunk dad, who is mean and belittling. He pressures Travis to play football and tells him what a loser he is. Travis buries himself online, where he connects in a chat room with Amelia, a girl who loves Bloodfall and is nice to him. A tiny bit of cheer in his very dark world.

5. Dill: Mom can't even afford her meds for her back pain, putting pressure on Dill to quit school, work full-time, and make money for the family (since it's all his fault that Dad is in prison). She attacks his friends because they aren't church-going perfect kids. Dill sees no future for himself, as he cannot stand up for himself because he has little self-esteem.

6. Lydia: As she talks to her parents, we see what a wonderful family she has, how lucky she is to have such an easy life. They give her a new laptop, and we watch Lydia, online, connected to very successful and famous people due to her blog. She texts with Dahlia, the girl she hopes to room with at NYU, if she can get in.

7. Dill: First day of school, and kids tease and torment him over his dad. They insult Lydia too, but she is fast with her wits and cuts them down to size. Dill wants to punch Tyson for his insults, but Lydia prevails. Point of scene: Dill feels like a loser, but Lydia believes in him and champions him.

8. Travis: works hard at the lumber mill. More texting with Amelia, who has an awful dad too. Travis (and the reader) learn the

important story about Dill's grandfather, who started handling snakes, and Dill's crazy dad, who is famous for snake-handling in his church. If you are chosen and faithful, you can handle vipers without getting bit, and you can drink poison and you won't die (something Dill's dad did often in church). This sets up Dill feeling he has bad blood and can't escape his family name and reputation.

9. **Key Scene #2 - Inciting Incident.** (18% mark) Dill: He's with Lydia at a coffee shop. She tries to persuade him to go to college. *Why is this the Inciting Incident? Because this is the first time Dill hears the suggestion that he go to college, the idea that he could actually leave this dead-end town and make something of himself. Up till now he has resolved that he will never leave. His mother wants him to stay in Forrestville forever and take care of her as penance for his crime. (For Dill to come into his essence by the end of the book, he must be able, ready, and willing to leave the town and the guilt behind, so this is why this scene is the moment his focus starts to shift, to move him toward his goal.)*

10. Lydia: Travis joins them in the coffee shop. Lydia starts writing her college entrance essay, ever focused on leaving, and insisting (to the boys' hurt) that there is nothing in this town worth staying for.

11. Dill: runs into a former church member, who attacks and blames Dill for his preacher dad being in jail. Dill goes to Lydia's house for dinner, sadly comparing his pathetic life with Lydia's wonderful parents and home life.

12. Travis: He texts Amelia, feeling happy that someone actually likes him. He and Dill are at Lydia's watching a documentary with her. They decide to go to the "Column" over at the bridge to write something memorable on it, to leave behind for future generations to read.

13. Dill: They sit up over the river and write their profound thoughts on the Column.

14. Lydia: She talks with her dad about what a dumb choice it was to raise her here. Dad reminds her that she has two great friends, and

she agrees. He tells her things about Travis's parents that she didn't know, inspiring empathy for Travis. She texts Dahlia, and they talk more about their New York plans.

15. Dill: He's with Lydia at the bookstore, buying his mom a birthday present. He flashes back to right before his dad got arrested, when he sang and played guitar in church. His dad had almost handed him a snake to handle, then changed his mind, implying Dill was unworthy and lacked faith, and that has plagued Dill ever since, making him doubt his own worthiness and impounding his doubts about his faith.

16. Travis: Dill asks if Travis's mom could make his own mom a birthday cake. She agrees, and Travis helps. But his dad comes in and ruins everything, drunk, calling Travis a fag. Travis retreats to his room and texts Amelia, who cheers him up.

17. **Key Scene #3 - First Pinch Point (30%).** Dill: gives Mom the cake and floats the idea of college to her. She gets furious and tells him absolutely not. He must stay in town and work full-time to support her until Dad gets out of prison. He redirects his anger at Lydia, who gave him the dumb idea to go to college. He knows he is trapped and can never leave. *I ID this as the first pinch point because, related to the goal of college, this is his first attempt to present his case to go to college, and his mom (the strong opposition in the story to this goal) says no. Here, true to the purpose of the pinch point, we see the full force of the opposition.*

18. Lydia: We read a long blog post she writes that shows both her knowledge of fashion and her disgust with her small-town life. She's at the library and spots Travis, who is texting someone and actually laughing—something she's never seen. She teases him and wants to know who the girl is.

19. **Key Scene #4 - Twist #1.** Dill: working at the market (his part-time job), he helps a little girl who falls off a mechanical pony. The mother, knowing who he is, screams at him and accuses him of trying to molest the girl (clearly, everyone in town thinks Dill is the pedophile and that his dad was innocent and framed by his lying son). Dill, shook up, goes to the library, reads Lydia's blog post (in

145

which she complains that she has no friends in this dumpy town), and gets angry at her (hurt that she is embarrassed to have him as a friend). She argues back challenging Dill for his choice to stay in town. She threatens to abandon him, and he feels panic. Lydia dumps him off at his house and drives away. (Lydia, in her persona, can't admit to having such pathetic friends as Dill and Travis to her thousands of online followers.) *I chose this as Twist #1 because suddenly Dill's only real support is yanked from him. Remember what Twist #1 is about? "Something new happens: a new ally, a friend becomes a foe. New info reveals a serious complication to reaching the goal. The protagonist must adjust in response to this setback." Dill's friend becomes a foe, and the incident with the little girl shows just how much Dill's life in his community is impacted by his decision to testify against his father, and more to come if he sticks around after graduation. In other words, his personal stakes and the weight of his choice is emphasized via this twist.*

20. Travis: texting Amelia, and they are getting close. Dill calls and asks Travis to help fix his mom's car. As Travis works on the car, he urges Dill to make up with Lydia.

21. Dill: goes to Lydia's and apologizes. Shares how his mother went ballistic over the college idea. Lydia tries to reason with him, then gives him her old laptop. Dill is stunned and thrilled. He talks with Lydia's dentist dad, who also plays guitar. Dill is encouraged by Lydia's dad taking an interest in him and being kind to him.

22. **Key Scene #5 - Midpoint.** Lydia: Dill and she are eating lunch at school, when the football creeps once again harass Dill. Lydia, once more, cuts them down to size. She texts her friends about college, working hard to fit in with the rich and elite. She starts to upload Dill's music videos that he's made of him playing and is stunned and impressed with his talent. **This shifts her feelings for him.** She tries to persuade Dill to enter the school talent contest, and via her online clout, his music videos start going viral. *This is the Midpoint even though it is in Lydia's POV. Here is where Dill realizes he has true talent, which hints at a possible future he never dreamed of—one in which he has self-worth. He steps over a threshold here. He begins his journey, committed to make something of his life beyond working at a market.*

23. **Key Scene #6 - Pinch Pont #2.** Dill practices for the show, then gets up on stage and performs. Though kids chide him, Lydia's smile gives him courage to surrender to his music. He wins. (*I would include this as part of the Midpoint, as a continuation of the above scene.*) Just as he's wondering how long this euphoria will last, not a week later his mom rails on him, dumping blame on him for Dad being in prison, again. She tells him he must by lying because he never handled the snakes (this motif weaves through the story). Lydia's dad drives Dill to see Dad in prison, and Dad does his usual berating and blaming of Dill. **But this time, as with his mother, Dill stands up and throws the truth at him.** His dad, disgusted, storms away. In the car, Dill breaks down, has a wonderful heart-to-heart with Lydia's dad. Dill is worried he has poisoned blood, but Dr. Blankenship reassures Dill, who says, "I really wish you were my dad." Doc answers: "I would be proud if you were my son." Dill is getting more validation that he does have worth—from someone he respects. *This is the second pinch point that revisits Dill facing off with his mom, but this time, though the opposition is even stronger and more pressing, Dill stands up to her.*

24. Travis: Lydia is driving Travis and Dill to the airport for a surprise. She won't say why. Through her various connections, she's arranged for the author of the Bloodfall series to spend a few hours with her "greatest fan." Travis is beside himself with excitement. They take Mr. Pennington for ice cream, where Travis plies him with questions. Pennington tells Travis he should start writing, and a spark inside Travis catches fire. "Something began to grow inside him . . . something that might be able to grow through the rocks and dirt that his father piled on him." Lydia gets Pennington to autograph a hardcover copy of a book for Travis. Exuberant, he goes home, only to face a drunk father who attacks him for missing work. They fight, and Dad grabs the book and starts ripping it. Travis falls to the floor to protect it as his dad beats him with a belt. Finally, something breaks inside Travis. He stands, faces Dad, and threatens him. "You lay a hand on me again, I'll break it off your arm." And "if you lay a hand on my mom again, I'll kill you." Dad kicks him out, so Travis kisses Mom and leaves.

25. Dill: Lydia had filled the laptop with music, which Dill loves. He hears a tap on his window and finds Travis. Determined to change his life, Travis asks Dill if he'd room with him after graduation, to which Dill agrees. Travis stays at Dill's house now. A moving ending when Travis sits alone in the car and weeps, and Dill watches from his house.

26. Lydia: Travis brings her his first story, wanting her opinion. She warns she will be brutal. She later checks the mail and finds she's been accepted to NYU!

27. Dill: After work, Lydia shows up and takes him to the coffee shop. She tells him the news, wanting him to be happy for her. But how can he? His heart is breaking.

28. Travis: sits by the river texting Amelia. She offers to meet him so they can read the new novel together. He is so happy. But then two meth heads drive up and rob him, then shoot him. Travis dies.

29. **Key Scene #7 - Twist #2.** Dill: He and Lydia can't reach Travis. They drive to where he said he'd be and see emergency vehicles. They go to the hospital, where they learn Travis has died. Dill weeps. When he goes home and his mom questions him, all she says is, "Was he saved?" *Clearly the big twist in the plot, which is "usually some reversal, betrayal, unforeseen complication." This surely meets that definition, right?*

30. Lydia: Two days later Dill is at her house. They talk about the killers who were caught, looking for money to buy drugs. They walk to Travis's funeral, where they meet Amelia and see Pennington has sent flowers and a very touching card.

31. Dill: He and Lydia are at Travis's grave talking about what Travis's life might have been had he lived. They have a deep talk about life, God, family. He shares his fear that he has the "snake poison" in his blood. *(I love this snake motif, because it's all about being worthy. Dill has been deemed unworthy because he could never hold the snakes, but his life, although deadly and poisonous, is something he courageously grabs with both hands and masters.)* Lydia tells him to be strong and promise to tell her if he ever considers suicide. He promises.

32. Lydia: Home from the funeral, she talks to Dad. He tries to console her. Her friend Dahlia texts about trivial things, and Lydia tells her a good friend just died. She realizes how wrong it was to be embarrassed about her true friends. She makes a step into her essence when she posts on her blog about Travis, her cowardice and shame, and how he was a true friend. She weeps.

33. Dill: in his room, depressed. Travis's mom shows up, gives him the staff. He sees her car is packed; she's leaving the drunk husband. His own mom comes in after, trying to cheer him up with religious platitudes, but it only sends him into deeper darkness.

34. Lydia: She calls Dill, waiting outside to take him to school, but he doesn't answer or come out. Frightened, she hurries inside him house and finds him. She urges him to come, but he won't, assuring her he'll be okay.

35. **Key Scene #8 – Dark Night.** Dill: sinks deeper into depression. Considers suicide. Stares at the river and decides to die. This is a literal "dark night of the soul" time for Dill.

36. Lydia: Dill shows up at her house because he promised he would tell her when he was about to kill himself. Talking with her, he knows now that, to survive, he must leave town, go to college. He's decided. Lydia and he pull an all-nighter, filling out college apps and writing essays. Her dad writes Dill a letter of rec.

37. Dill: strokes her hand (1 paragraph)

38. Lydia: She enjoys it (1 paragraph)

39. Dill: kisses her (1 paragraph)

40. Lydia: Their first kiss interrupted by her mom coming to her room. They laugh; they're happy and hopeful. Lydia is glad Dill is cheering up and tells him his music videos are getting thousands of views. They kiss more and laugh about how they are really complicating their lives.

41. Dill: They agree to keep their closeness low-key as school wraps up, aware they are going separate ways. Dill quits working at the market and instead works for Lydia's dad through summer, and through the dental company gets good counseling and antidepressants. He gets accepted at the state U he'd hoped for, and Lydia, excited for him, drives him to the campus to see where he'll be attending school. He's enthralled, and then a student recognizes him from his music video and gushes praise. The future is bright. When he gets home, he plays a song he wrote for her.

42. Lydia: Has a wonderful, warm exchange with her parents when she gets home, as well as a heart-to-heart with Mom about being in love with Dill. We see how much Lydia has come into her essence through all this.

43. **Key Scene #9 – Big Climax.** Dill: Mom gets home. He wasn't going to tell her about college until the day before leaving, but now he decides to stand up and face her. Instead of lying, he tells the truth (coming into his essence here). She takes her virulent stand, throwing every accusation and pushing every guilt button, but he does not budge on his decision. She walks out. Dill thinks: "If you're going to live, you might as well do painful, brave, and beautiful things." *This is the climax because the visible goal for the book, however subtle, is Dill going off to college. So this big, final standoff, facing his opposition, shows him reaching his goal. Nothing will stop him now.*

44. Lydia: They're at school and decide to go to the prom, but make it the most pathetic, ridiculous prom night ever. They dress silly, eat at a cheap diner and order a yucky meal, talk about Travis and how they miss him, and cry.

45. Dill: They ride an old bike contraption to the prom, discuss leaving town, college. "We made it," they realize, but Dill feels guilty about Travis. He hopes he is watching them and is happy for them.

46. Lydia: At the prom, kids scowl, but they are Brave and Beyond All This.

47. Dill: They bike back to Lydia's after prom and kiss. They play in the sprinklers and look at the stars, laughing. Dill holds this moment with her in his arms.

48. Dill: They sit at Travis's grave. Lydia is leaving tomorrow. They say good-bye to Travis, then to the Column, "listening to the river wear its way deeper into the Earth, the way people wear grooves into each other's hearts."

49. Lydia: drives Dill home, they sing songs. She encourages him and tells him he is not his father or grandfather. He does not have their poison. "Their darkness is not your darkness."

50. Lydia: They kiss.

51. Dill: tells Lydia: "You saved me." Lydia says, "You saved yourself." He gives her his music CD. She drives away after he says, "I love you."

52. Lydia: driving to NY to college. She stops in a shop Dill recommended, feeling bad she didn't tell Dill she loved him. We see how much she's changed, and how much Dill has changed her.

53. **Key Scene #10 – Resolution.** Dill: visits Dad in prison. Dad accuses Dill of hateful things, abandoning his mom, being selfish. But as with his mother, the mean words slide off him. He stands up for himself and no longer feels cowed. Instead, he looks upon Dad with pity. When he's ready to leave for college, his music has really taken off, and a famous performer asks if she can record one of his songs. He tells his mother she was wrong. God did envision a better life for him and sent people to him to give him courage and show him his real choices. He asks if she's at all proud of him. She answers: "I don't know." Then she admits she's scared of being alone. Her tough shell cracks. Dill tells her he's scared too. He hugs her and leaves for college, feeling finally free for the first time. *The resolution really takes place over many of these last scenes as Dill wraps up his life in Forrestville.*

I hope this foray into the summary of *The Serpent King* gave you some insights into how a novel with little plot and emphasis on character can still be structured with the first layer of ten key scenes. The author clearly gave Dill a goal at the right spot in the novel, and the MDQ (major dramatic query) is very apparent: Will Dill have the courage to leave his stifling small town and go to college and brave a new world?

When you formulate your MDQ, it helps you set that visible goal. The MDQ is the "yes or no" question you ask of your protagonist at the start of your novel. This question is answered at the climax of the story. In fact, there are two MDQs, and both are answered at the climax scene. In addition to a visible goal, there is a spiritual or emotional one. The spiritual MDQ for Dill would be something like this: "Will Dill rise above his family 'curse' and believe he really is a valuable, worthy person?" This is, as stated earlier, all about coming into his essence, his true nature, and accepting that true nature with open arms.

We also saw visible goals for both Lydia and Travis. They too wanted to break from their small town and the emotional binds. Travis had a similar emotional MDQ as Dill: he had to stand up to his domineering father once and for all, and he came into his essence fully before he died. Lydia's character arc didn't involve a change in visible goal; she'd planned on college all along. But what changed drastically was her perspective—of herself and those around her. Her change, to me, is the most dramatic.

So take the time to do this exercise. Break down and summarize a few novels in your genre. Identify those ten key scenes, then scrutinize the other scenes and locate those that might make up the second layer, then the third. Yes, you are working backward because when you work on your novel, you're starting with nothing. But this deconstructing will instruct you.

And that leads me to your assignment!

* * *

Your assignment: Yep, go through the above scene summary outline and figure out the *next layer*. Since the romance and subplot methods don't apply here, use the action-reaction method. Identify the next most important ten scenes—the ones that are transitional. These might be the reaction/processing of a key event or the decision to act (new direction).

Once you do that, think about the next layer and how those (perhaps) smaller scenes help bind the story together and facilitate the smooth flow of the plot's unfolding. These smaller scenes are the glue (the sand) that fills in those spaces between major scenes.

Extra assignment (and this may help you a lot!): Create a chart of your 20 key scenes, one sentence per scene. Note why you chose these as key scenes. Print it out and use it as reference material. (Why not print out all the charts and keep them in a folder?) Put them in chronological order, but number them according to the layers as shown in previous examples in this book.

Here's an example:

Scene #1 Setup: Dill. Lydia picks him and Travis up the day before school starts to go clothes shopping.

Scene #11: Dill visits Dad in prison, where we see how awful he's treated and blamed. **Sets up his relationship with his father and his place in his "world."**

Scene #2 Inciting Incident: Lydia suggests Dill go to college and get away from Forrestville.

Scene #12: Dill with Lydia at bookstore: **establishes the key backstory of Dill's father and grandfather, handling snakes, Dill's "failure" and unworthiness.**

Scene #3 First Pinch Point: Dill mentions college to Mom, who goes ballistic.

I hope you're getting the hang of layering!

Chapter 16: Example of a Well-Structured Novel

Brilliance by Marcus Sakey is the first installment in a sci-fi thriller that serves as a perfect example of a well-structured novel. Sakey lays out his scenes almost to the page in line with the Ten Key Scene Chart. And, as I hope you'll see as you go through the scene summary, this framework makes for a terrific novel.

Since 1980, 1 percent of the population of the world has been born with special abilities. Called abnorms, these gifted people now number in the millions, and, as expected, some have used their abilities to wreak havoc on society, crashing the stock markets and committing crimes. Tensions have reached their peak between abnorms and normals, as violence is escalating, much of it fomented by a man called John Smith.

Sakey starts right in high action in the novel, setting up his protagonist, Nick Cooper, a federal agent, on the run after Alex Vasquez, a coder who the Feds believe work for Smith. A deadly attack is in the works, and Cooper must capture Alex and get her code.

The kicker for this "stop the terrorist" plot is that Cooper is an abnorm, using his uncanny abilities to "read" people in service of the government—which often involves murder. And when his young daughter, Kate, is clearly showing signs of being a tier-one abnorm herself, the stakes shoot sky high.

Note that Sakey divides the book into three parts: The Hunter, The Hunted, and The Rogue. These are fairly equal-sized sections, and they succinctly identify Cooper's character arc. He starts off as the hunter, and we watch him hunt down the enemy. At the (very early) Midpoint, he is now the hunted. And by the end of the book, he's changed sides fundamentally. Not that he's become a terrorist but that his essence is with his people, the abnorms, instead of with normals, which prior was his whole world.

I mentioned at the start of *Layer Your Novel* that the story you tell may require you to fudge the positioning of the key scenes for best storytelling. You shouldn't try to fit square pegs into round holes. And this is what Sakey does by having a very clear, definitive Midpoint much earlier than usual. But he didn't need to spend half the novel getting Cooper to that Midpoint "door of no return." Once he becomes the hunted, he's all-in and there's no turning back, and the unfolding developments getting to the climax and resolution carry the bulk of the scenes, which is perfectly fine.

So again, don't get your boxers in a bunch trying to make every scene fit to the exact percentage mark. But be sure those key scenes are in the right place and serving their needed purpose.

I hope you'll study this breakdown carefully—because I believe it will teach you much about solid novel structure and why these ten key scenes are essential to great storytelling.

Brilliance
By Marcus Sakey

1. **Key Scene #1 – Setup. Part 1 – The Hunter.** Cooper arrives in San Antonio after chasing Alex Vasquez for nine days. He goes into a hotel bar, finds her there, and chats about the recent bombings, about abnorms. She realizes she's caught. He grills her about the code, tries to get her to turn herself in. She runs, he chases her to the roof. She's disgusted that he's an abnorm and hunting his own kind. She agrees there's a war coming and tells him he has to pick a side. She then dives headfirst off the roof. *[Excellent setup of character, his work, his dedication and personality, the stakes, the situation between abnorms and normals.]*

2.   Cooper's team (He works for DAR—Department of Analysis and Response) takes Alex's body back to DC. Cooper calls Drew Peters, head of Equitable Services (ES), his superior, to tell them Vasquez is dead. It's clear Alex had to have a contact—she wouldn't have been able to execute the code. Cooper visits his ex-wife, Natalie, and his kids—Todd, nine, and Kate, four. She's worried about Kate, who's showing signs of being an abnorm. Nick reminds her that kids aren't tested until eight years of age. If Kate tests positive, she'd be taken from her family and put in an academy. Nick gets a call from Quinn, one of his team members. Alex's brother, Bryan, a normal, has been brought in for questioning and claims he and Alex were working for John Smith, public enemy #1, who Cooper is after. He says there's an attack imminent.

3.   Cooper arrives at DAR headquarters and discusses the details of the case with Peters. We see his rival in the office—Dickinson—who is trying to take over Cooper's role in this pursuit of John Smith. Dickinson is already interrogating Bryan, but Peters makes clear Cooper's in charge and he trusts Cooper (establishing their deep close relationship) even though he's an abnorm.

4.   Cooper learns from Bryan that he's to meet with a contact tomorrow to pass on the code to him. Even though Bryan's a normal, he's a patriot for the abnorm rebel cause. Letting Bryan believe his sister, Alex, is still alive and will see her if he cooperates, he agrees to being part of a sting to entrap the contact.

5.   Cooper and Quinn discuss the logistics of setting up the sting. Cooper wants to understand how a terrorist like Smith could happen. While waiting for the team to assemble, he decides to do some research.

6.   **Key Scene #2 - Inciting Incident (10% mark).** Cooper visits one of the academies that house the children who are tested as top-tier abnorms. He was born long before the academies were set up. This very important scene shows Cooper alarmed at what is done to these children, who are taken away from their families at age eight and never see them again during their ten-year stay. Since abnorms are considered highly dangerous, they are indoctrinated

to distrust one another and bond with their mentor, and they have a chip in them that "bugs" them and records everything they say and do. The environment is the perfect ground for all kinds of psychosis and isolationism as the mentors manipulate these vulnerable children. This shatters Cooper's previously assumption that the academies were to help the gifted master their abilities for good. *[This is clearly the Inciting Incident, as these shocking truths are the impetus for the goal and related decisions Cooper makes for the rest of the book.]*

7. Cooper and Quinn are at the location of the sting—outdoors. Bryan tells of his desire to help unite normals and abnorms. Cooper feels guilty lying to Bryan about his sister, but he is on a righteous mission. He and his team murder to save the innocent. They watch for the contact, a man puts coins into a newspaper dispenser, and Bryan explodes.

8. Back at DAR, they review the footage of the explosion, trying to figure out who detonated the bomb in the newspaper box. Cooper realizes the bomb must have been detonated via cell phone, then remembers a beautiful woman talking on a cell phone near the scene. Team starts tracing phone calls made in the area to see if any are connected to Bryan.

9. Cooper reviews old tapes showing Smith walking into a restaurant and shooting a senator in the face. Violence erupted, and Smith's group killed seventy-three people—the beginning of Smith's reign of terror. While most people want to find a way for abnorms and normals to live together in peace, Smith is determined to start a war of huge proportion. What disturbs Cooper most is understanding how the academies are responsible for creating monsters like Smith. He is determined his daughter will never go to one. As he's heading out the next morning, his ex calls, sobbing. Something terrible has happened.

10. Cooper hurries to see Natalie. She says officials are going to take Kate for testing, even though she is four. She shows uncanny signs of being a tier one. And that means an academy—Cooper and Natalie will never see their daughter again. Now the horror of the situation hits home, and while Cooper believes the work he is

doing is essential and right, he knows the way abnorms are being treated is wrong. His fear has now turned to rage.

11. Cooper goes to ES and talks to Drew Peters. He tells Peters his daughter is probably tier one and that she's to be tested. He begs Peters to prevent this. Peters says he can't. Cooper knows there has to be a way to protect his daughter. That matters to him more than anything. Peters says the best way to help Kate is to do his job. That he's out there trying to prevent a war.

12. **25% mark – goal fixed.** Cooper knows there must be a way to protect Kate. He knows ES wants Smith more than anything. **He figures if he delivers Smith, he'll be in a position to deal.** The team, after reviewing all info, determines the beautiful woman on the cell phone at the scene was the bomber. They follow a lead to a Dusty Evans in NJ. A gunfight ensues. Quinn is shot but okay. Cooper gets two men in custody. In the van, he presses them to talk, tell what they know about the impending attack. They won't cooperate. Cooper throws one man out of the car, where he's run over and killed. Cooper then turns to Dusty and tells him to talk or he's next.

13. **Key Scene #3 - First Pinch Point (28% mark).** Cooper is in Manhattan, where the big attack is to take place. Due to a brilliant named Epstein, the stock market crashed and shut down some years back. Now there's a new exchange, and the first IPO is being offered today, finally getting the market back on its feet. The city is packed. Dusty revealed five bombs have been planted. Cooper races against the clock to get to the bombs to disarm them, then spots the woman bomber and decides to chase after her, assuming she's to detonate them. He sees her pull out a phone and attacks her. She pleads for him to let her go, that he doesn't understand . . . then the explosion occurs. [*This huge explosion shows the power and force of the opposition, Cooper's nemesis—perfect pinch point.*]

14. Cooper, dazed amid destruction, comes to in an Army triage tent. Well enough to stumble out, he searches for the female bomber. The city is full of bodies, and, in horror, he watches replays of the explosion on the 3D billboards, giving tangible proof of the threat of John Smith and need to stop him at all costs.

15. **Key Scene #5 – Midpoint [note, this comes at the 35% mark instead of the 50%, with Part 2 a bit longer than part 1].** Cooper stumbles to Peters's home. Cooper spells it out (his goal): DAR wants Smith, and Cooper will deliver him . . . on one condition. His idea is crazy: he will act the turncoat and claim responsibility for the attack, and will then be DAR's enemy. Only Peters and Natalie would know. Peters thinks this is a bad idea but Cooper is adamant. The stakes couldn't be higher. He goes to visit Natalie and tells her what's about to happen. He will not see her or his children for a long time—maybe never again. She's horrified, but he tells her: "If I do this, Kate won't be tested. *Ever*. That was my price. She won't be taken from us. She'll never see the inside of an academy."

16. **Part 2 – The Hunted.** It's six months after the big explosion. Cooper has been undercover, getting into his role, hoping he's proving he's on Smith's side and an enemy of the DAR. And the DAR has been hunting him down. He's finally met with someone who might get him close to Smith. He brings smuggler Zane some tech, and he makes a deal for Zane to give Cooper a new name, face, and ID.

17. Cooper returns to his hotel, where he's living and known as Mr. Eliot. He reflects on how easy it's been to be a criminal (processing scene) and how much he's missed his family. But he's determined to see this through.

18. **Key Scene #4 - Twist #1. [Instead of coming before the Midpoint, this comes after.]** He's on the Chicago El Train platform, waiting for Zane. Suddenly, he sees the beautiful female bomber. She has a gift of moving nearly unnoticed, and now she's ordering him to get up, a pistol aimed at him. She blames him for killing an abnorm she knows. He defends himself, saying Vargas was a murderer. Then the place fills with DAR agents, including Quinn and Dickinson. Zane sold him out. They're both in trouble and run. He detonates a flash he'd hidden in his shoe to temporarily blind the agents and the two get away by jumping atop a moving train, though the woman is reluctant to go with Cooper. The twist: Cooper, surprised, has found a key ally to Smith and is with her.

19. Cooper and the woman get to Nick's hotel and talk about the conflict and stakes. She's also in trouble now, having been seen with Cooper, and her side will think she's compromised (because Cooper isn't yet trusted by the Smith faction). So they will team up. Epstein, the brilliant who crashed the stock market, took over half of Wyoming and built a compound there, a high-security safe haven for abnorms that the government can't touch, and that's where they'll head. There, Cooper can get safe (his cover story) and he'll get her there safely, where she can be vetted. But they first need new IDs.

20. They go out to acquire a rare drug to give as a gift to a friend the woman, who Cooper has learned is named Shannon, feels can help them. They sneak into a hospital, steal a doc's ID, and Shannon gets into the dispensary to get the drug. They're almost caught.

21. At Samantha's house, Cooper meets an eccentric, rich, powerful drug addict. She has a gift of becoming whatever men want, and she works Cooper. But she is close to Smith, and Shannon asks Sam to tell Smith they're coming. Cooper has proved today he's no spy—the DAR was clearly trying to kill him, so he wins the women's confidence. Sam tries to seduce Cooper, but when he refuses, she kicks him and Shannon out. They talk about how Sam is really a prostitute—the academy ruined her and she's now a pathetic drug addict because of her mentor. Drives home, once more, how dangerous the academies are and what's at stake for Cooper and his little girl.

22. Cooper and Shannon discuss their gifts. He learns Smith told her and others in his group not to trust Cooper. He's surprised to hear he's been on Smith's radar and Smith almost had his car blown up. Cooper tells Shannon he knows someone who can give them IDs and papers. They go to the man's sweatshop, where abnorms are working to pay off the new IDs he creates for them.

23. They go to Chinatown to stay with Lee Chen. Chinatown houses countless abnorms, where the children are cherished and raised under the radar of ES. DAR has a hard time getting into Chinatown's web and so this is a kind of safe haven for these children. At Chen's house he watches the children play

extraordinary mind games. They are truly brilliant, happy, and innocent: showing Cooper what the world should be like—embracing these gifts and gifteds. The two are given a room to sleep in, and Cooper misses his kids. But he's doing this for him: for a changed world that must come.

24. **Key Scene #6 - Pinch Pont #2.** They pick up the IDs from the sweatshop guy, then as they return to Chinatown to thank the Chens, a big DAR attack is in progress. They run, hide, can't do anything but watch as the Chens and their brilliant young daughter are dragged out of their place, bags put over their heads, and thrown into a vehicle. Cooper is horrified: this is all his fault. They've somehow followed him via CCTVs all over the city. Now he's more enraged. He must get to Wyoming, to John Smith, and end this. *[This pinch point hits even more powerfully than the city attack because it's personal. He liked these people and admired them, and now their world is destroyed because of him. The enemy looks even worse when shown through a personal lens and drives home to Cooper how much danger his daughter is in.]*

25. They're driving, get to the border of the compound, to an outlying town. Get through the first inspection. Reach Shannon's apartment, where they'll stay for now. They go out drinking and have dinner to celebrate getting this far. They are getting closer and enjoying each other's company. We see Cooper changing the way he sees the world.

26. Next day, they arrive in the compound, go through security, and get in to see Epstein. But he's a hologram. They talk with him in the presence of a highly gifted ten-year-old, Millie, who reveals when they are lying or telling the truth. Then Cooper is told to go with Millie, who takes him down an elevator to a basement. She points toward a dark room at the end of the hallway.

27. **Key Scene #7 - Twist #2.** Cooper goes inside this amazing room of 3D data filling the air and meets the real Epstein. The hologram is his brother, who was said to have died years ago. This real Epstein hides in his data, brilliant and able to see endless connections and possibilities of outcomes. A high-processing computer mind. Of course he knows who Cooper really is and

why he's really come, getting Cooper to tell him that he's come to kill Smith. Epstein is glad. Smith threatens Epstein's beautiful and smoothly run compound, as well as his sublime vision of the future world he's trying to create—a world that is safe for abnorms. But Smith is threatening everything Epstein believes in. His data proves Smith must die ASAP or all will be ruined. So he will help Cooper reach his goal. *[Perfect twist: a supposed enemy is now his main ally and help to reach his goal.]*

28. Cooper is given a briefcase when he leaves Epstein. He and Shannon have dinner, then he packs and leaves for a cabin in the woods, where Smith will be, meeting a woman to have some private time. He calls Peters from a phone in a car dealership—first time since he went rogue. He's angry about Chen's family, demands Peters fix that. Tells Peters tonight he's killing Smith and if anything goes south, Peters must promise Kate is safe and will never be tested; he does. He says, "Whatever happens, I'll take care of your family." Cooper has sacrificed much and Peters knows it.

29. Cooper scouts out the cabin. There are guards, but he slowly gets past them, some close calls. But he makes it up onto the second-floor balcony just outside the bedroom where he spotted Smith. Tension and stakes are high. Pistol in hand, he slides the door open and slips inside.

30. Cooper sneaks through rooms, no one there. Then comes into an office where flat screens are playing over and over the attack where Smith and his team killed seventy-three people. But . . . as he watches the videos replay over and over, Cooper sees things that are incongruent. He's seen this footage many times, but now he's seeing the incident from new angles and he realizes the man who is ID'd as Smith can't actually be there . . . then the door opens. Cooper aims his gun at Smith, who says, "Hello, Cooper. I'm not John Smith."

31. Cooper wants to pull the trigger, but Shannon is suddenly there, aiming a shotgun at Cooper! Smith tells him he can pull the trigger but hasn't he started figuring out the truth? Cooper says, "The video is fake." Smith says yes, he had met with the senator, but

way earlier. He wasn't there at the massacre. Smith and Shannon convince Cooper to put down his gun. He does, and she puts hers down too. Smith explains his terrorist persona was invented and faked. After that attack, Smith became the target. Shocked, Cooper pieces it together: how the DAR needed a reason to exist, funding, the power to kill . . . Drew Peters orchestrated it all, for his own purposes: to get rid of abnorms. His boss and friend . . . who sent him to get Smith. Which horrifies Cooper as he thinks of all the people he murdered for Peters. He runs out.

32. **Part 3 – The Rogue. Key Scene #8 – Dark Night.** Cooper runs out into the night, the guards letting him go. He's in shock, processing this horrific truth: that Peters is the enemy. There is no denying it; the pieces all fit. ES has tremendous power over the world because of the evil they've done. Cooper sees now that he is the terrorist, not Smith. Shannon finds him. He's in grief. He talks about a brilliant doctor he murdered, realizing now the man was innocent and had so much to contribute to making the world better. This is the flood of pain and guilt—a truly dark night moment. He wants to die, but Shannon says that cowardly. Instead he can reveal the truth to the world, be a hero. There is evidence that can be revealed to expose Peters and ES. They make love.

33. Cooper and Smith climb a mountain peak and talk privately. Smith explains the options and convinces Cooper he has to find the proof that damns and exposes Peters and his agency's evil. He reveals he sent Shannon to get him, making Cooper doubt Shannon's honesty and sincerity.

34. Cooper flies to DC, about to risk all to find the evidence he needs. He knows Peters would hide something as insurance. During the flight he narrows down where it might be hid, then figures it out.

35. Goes to the cemetery near Peters's house, where the director's wife's mausoleum is. Cooper breaks in, spots a security/alarm box. Knows Peters has now been alerted to Cooper's invasion. Cooper searches the crypt and finds a data stick, runs out. Agents chase and fire at him; he fires back and kills his first DAR agent. Runs into Quinn, convinces him to let him go, swearing he's not guilty. Quinn reluctantly lets Cooper run.

36. Cooper now is convinced Peters is the enemy, having sent his team to kill him for taking the data stick. Cooper calls Natalie, but Dickinson answers. ES has his family, and Dickinson is in cahoots with Peters. Cooper holes up in a bathroom and watches the video—shocking evidence that makes him realize Peters will not let Cooper's family live. The stakes shoot up even higher.

37. Cooper calls Quinn. They meet at a pub. Wary, Quinn lets Cooper tell the whole story, and then watches the video showing the now-president of the US meeting with Peters and setting up the attack at the restaurant, the setup of Smith as the terrorist, and their plan to benefit from creating a war. Shocked, Quinn joins with Cooper. Then Shannon shows up to take a stand at his side. His two allies have come to his aid in the eleventh hour. Cooper finally feels a spark of hope.

38. Cooper calls Peters. Big standoff. Cooper lays out the deal: He'll give Peters the uncopied data stick if Peters hands Cooper his family. Someplace they both agree on. Cooper and Quinn talk. Peters will bring a force, no doubt. But Quinn is an inside man. He goes to get supplies. Shannon and Cooper wait at Quinn's place. They have a heart-to-heart. Admit feelings for each other, sorry for the mistrust.

39. **Key Scene #9 – Big Climax.** The three are atop a parking garage with weapons and other gear. Cooper calls Peters. Peters gives the street name and Cooper, with Quinn's prompting, gives the address to meet. He gives Peters ten minutes, then hangs up. They go to the building, head into the security office using Quinn's DAR creds. They fight guards, get control of the room. Inject guards with sedatives. They put in earpieces, and Quinn views the security feeds. They watch Cooper's family come in the entrance. Cooper is emotionally upended at seeing his family after six months. Men are with the family, including Peters and Dickinson, who shoots a janitor. Cooper almost rushes out but Shannon holds him back. The family and men go up the elevator, stop at fifth floor, Natalie and kids get out. Shooters surround them as Peters goes up in the elevator. Cooper must be at that meeting on the tenth floor, sends the others to get his family. Cooper goes to the conference room and faces Peters and Dickinson. Another

standoff. Quinn talks in the earpiece, ID'ing the room the family is in. Shannon says she's on it. Cooper puts down the gun. Peters asks where the drive is, scoffing at Peters saying he'll deliver the family safe if he turns it over. Peters tells the guard remotely to kill Cooper's son. Cooper gives him the drive. The monitor shows Shannon attacking the guard about to kill the family. Cooper hides; Dickinson shoots. Peters runs out with the drive. No word from Shannon. Dickinson tells him the family is dead—Shannon too. With nothing to lose, Cooper attacks and kills Dickinson. Shannon has rescued the family; they're in the elevator but the troops are coming. A helicopter is coming. Cooper races to the roof. Cooper attacks Peters, then tosses him off the roof.

40. **Key Scene #10 – Resolution.** Cooper gets to a park, waiting to rendezvous. The streets are filled with law enforcement and DAR, but Peters is dead, so Cooper knows there will be confusion. He gets ready to release the video feed incriminating the president and Peters to the whole world via the internet. He thinks of how he could just threaten to leak it and blackmail the president, become the head of ES and make the proper changes for a better world. Naw . . . He presses Send. Truth over power. He goes to a safe house and reunites with family and Shannon. Shannon leaves, the family is safe. The world, for now, is safe. But he has a lot of work still to do . . .

I hope you see what a terrifically structured novel this is. As with most great thrillers, there are lots of twists—not just the two major ones in the first layer of scenes. And so, the second layer is made up of both the action-reaction-processing-decision scenes and the new twists, interspersed to build the action to the climax.

Sakey, appropriately, resolves the plot goal in the climax, yet leaves wide open the bigger goal—to change the world and make it safe for his children—for the next installments in the series (and I'm ordering them today!). Regardless of how many books you have in a series, each one must have an immediate visible goal for the protagonist that is resolved satisfyingly at the climax.

And, you'll notice, the author gets "in quick, out quick," not spending more than a few pages in this reunion with family and wrap-up of the story. What parts will Cooper's new allies—Shannon, Smith, and Quinn—play? We'll have to read book 2 and see.

In just the right places we see the force of the opposition (at the key pinch points). Sakey nicely sets up the early tension with Dickinson, along with the big red herring in his close relationship with Peters.

I'd planned to insert the scene summary below and identify the second layer of key scenes, but, by now, you should be an expert on this. So . . .

* * *

Your assignment: Identify the second layer of *Brilliance*—scenes 11-20. Find the important scenes that impact Cooper emotional and shift his worldview (such as the scene with Samantha, the prostitute, and Lee Chan's family). Find the other big twists, such as when Cooper watches the conflicting news feeds in the cabin, showing Smith couldn't have been at the restaurant attack. The big moments of plot and character change are those pebbles that go in the jar after the ten big rocks.

Once you've chosen your second layer (maybe copy and print out the scene summary so you can mark it up with highlighters), figure out the next layer of connective scenes: those processing scenes that are the glue that holds the story together. I bet after that, you could find the next ten, and the next . . .

Chapter 17: The Not-So-Perfect Novels

I know I risk the ire of some readers of this book by even suggesting any best seller is flawed. As I said, I'm not doing this from some arrogant perspective, thinking I'm a much better writer than these authors. My purpose in pointing out these flaws is to elucidate.

I truly believe novels are better when they're structured well. When they meet reader expectations of good storytelling. Be mad at me if you like, but I hope you'll stick with me and learn some valuable insights by these examinations.

The first book I want to look at is Gilly MacMillan's best-seller *The Perfect Girl*. It's labeled as literary suspense genre, but it not at all a literary suspense. It reads clearly, to me, as YA in writing style, voice, and level of sophistication. The protagonist is a teen, and while there are adult POVs, it's young Zoe's story, and the focus is on her response to all that occurs and her resultant actions. The book is written in multiple first-person accounts, which is very popular these days and provides an intimate look into various characters' heads.

The chapters are short and easy to read, and the plot is skimpy, focusing narrowly on the events of one evening, without the usual cast of possible suspects and red herrings you normally find in a mystery.

The novel has an awkward structure with the way it skips around in time. I personally find this irritating and unnecessary; the story could easily be told in chronological order. Everyone is recounting the events of Sunday night forward except Sam, the lawyer, who, for some reason, is placed in time the next day and is mostly just thinking of the past. And he has a few scenes in the beginning (which aren't all that needed) and then . . . none for a long while. The backstory fills the reader in on Zoe's accident and trial, and anything important in those scenes could be revealed via Zoe's scenes. I would leave him out of the story altogether except as a bit part, if even that.

There are a lot of chapters of backstory, which I also feel weakens the novel tremendously. It's telling instead of showing, and while somewhat effective because of the first-person POV accounts, stories (IMO) are always much better when shown—when the events play out in real time for readers to watch and experience. I also find the characters' emotional reactions often lacking in a big way.

In my 2016 analyses of twenty-six best-selling novels' first pages on my blog Live Write Thrive, I noted that a lot of hugely popular novelists get away with breaking expected structure and the "rules" we writers are told to obey. Many of these authors pack their opening scenes with explanation and narrative and backstory instead of "showing" their scenes in present action. And many of those novels are decidedly boring.

Yet, because these authors have a ginormous fan base, they can often get away with ignoring or dissing structure and the typical expectations of readers of their genre. Fans will often tolerate these infractions and plod through such books—maybe even enjoy them. Some fans will patiently slog through boring chapters hoping their favorite authors will eventually get things rolling, trusting the novel will get interesting at some point. Maybe a few fans fall by the wayside. Do these authors really care? I have no idea. But I care.

My argument is that every book an author writes should be terrific, and making the excuse that "I'm under tight deadline" or that readers won't mind poorly developed stories is inexcusable.

The Perfect Girl promises a suspenseful murder mystery, but I found it lacking suspense throughout. Having those ten key scenes in the right places would cover a multitude of sins. But the lack thereof is the symptom of a bigger problem: the thin plot. Not a whole lot happens in the novel, and what action there is lacks tension and high drama. We have a murder scene and practically no investigation.

You'll notice I leave out the second pinch point—it's not there. While it's set up that Barlow is the "opposition" at the right point in the story, it turns out there really isn't any clear opposition in this novel. I hope you'll see how this creates a big structural flaw. What we end up with here are a lot of scenes before the climax that lack tension and build.

Here's a summary of the plot:

Zoe Maisey, seventeen, is a music prodigy in Bristol, England, but her career derailed when she caused an accident that left three classmates dead. After serving time in The Unit, her mother insisted she and Zoe keep that bit of past secret from everyone—including the mom's new husband.

True to murder-mystery form, the novel opens with the mention of the death of Zoe's mom, and what follows is the playing out of events leading up to that death. In this story, we don't find the usual murder-mystery construct—an investigation to learn "who-dunnit."

Mystery novels usually rely on the murder as the Inciting Incident. As such, it often plays out in the first scene, which is also the setup scene. But not always. In the runaway best seller *The Girl on the Train*, while the short intro paragraph paints a sketchy picture of someone being (possibly) murdered, the actual event of the murder doesn't come into the story for many chapters. This novel, too, has a different Inciting Incident, due to the way the plot is structured. But the quality of the writing and structure of the two novels couldn't be more different.

As with the other novel examples, the POV character is noted at the start of each scene summary.

The Perfect Girl
By Gilly MacMillan

1. **Key Scene #1 – Setup.** Zoe, 17. Sunday. About to play piano at a church, very stressed. First time performing since she got out of jail; parents, Maria and Philip, had always expected perfection. She's with her stepbrother, Lucas, and they perform a brilliant duet on the piano. While they're playing shouting erupts. Zoe tells us that it's the beginning of the end, because "six hours later, my mother is dead."

2.   Sam, lawyer. Monday morning. Having affair with married Tessa, Zoe's aunt. He'd worked on Zoe's case. Gets call from his office: Zoe is there and says her mom is dead and wants to see her. She's with her uncle, Richard, Tessa's husband.

3.   Tessa, night of the concert. She's a vet. Her husband drinks. She thinks she needs to resist seeing Sam after the concert.

4.   **Key Scene #2 - Inciting Incident [or so it appears].** Zoe. Sunday night—continuation of her first scene. Lucas stops playing. A man in the aisle rages "It's a travesty." Zoe recognizes him as a father of one of the dead classmates: Barlow. Her mom tries to calm Barlow as Zoe flees the stage in fear. She leaves with her mom as Lucas stays and plays. They pass the cemetery and see a plaque to the man's dead daughter. Her mom reassures her everything will be all right, and Zoe wishes she had asked her mom if she was all right. *[It seems that the opposition is being shown here, but Barlow really has no real role in the story.]*

5.   Sam, Monday morning, cont'd. Recalls meeting Zoe. He'd been sent to represent her after the accident, and she refused to have her mother in the room with her. All backstory.

6.   Tessa, Sunday night, cont'd. She's filming the recital and sees the man in the aisle. Recounts from her POV. Barlow, the father, weeps as Zoe and mom hurries out. We learn that Chris is Maria's new husband, and that Zoe's family is now living a hundred miles from the previous town, names changed, hoping to be somewhat anonymous. Tessa doesn't know how Barlow found Zoe.

7.   Zoe. Sunday night, cont'd. She and Mom arrive home to find the Russian babysitter with a boyfriend. Katya takes care of the "miracle" baby that Maria and Chris had: Grace. Mom goes upstairs with baby and the boy leaves. Zoe worries about Chris grilling her and Mom about Barlow and the outburst (since they have no idea about the accident).

8.   Sam, Monday, cont'd. He wakes Tessa up to tell her her sister is dead. She dresses and heads out to Maria's house, to see to the baby, telling Sam to tend to Zoe.

9. Zoe, Sunday night, cont'd. Her mom is upstairs, and Zoe is anxious to talk to her before Lucas and Chris arrive. After a quick tense face-off with her and Katya, Zoe checks her phone app to see what "people" are up to. She gets a message: "Did you think you could stay hidden forever?"

10. Tessa, Sunday night, cont'd. She arranges to take Lucas and Chris home. Thinks about how Maria's marriage fell apart, then she moved to Bristol to be near Tessa, and got a job at the university. Father blamed the piano for Zoe's being bullied and the subsequent accident. Recounts how Maria met Chris, whose first wife died of an illness. Lucas asks if Zoe's all right. She reassures but reveals nothing.

11. Sam, Monday morning, cont'd. Backstory recounting what Sam learned about Zoe's accident: she was drunk, driving, and the three others in the car died.

12. Zoe, Sunday night cont'd. Talks about Panop: the social app that kids use to troll and harass. Lucas sends her a message on it: "Check your email." She does. There's a PDF he's sent entitled "What I know." She reads part of it. It's in screenplay form. It tells a bit of Lucas's life—his mother dying, his father's career—before Chris met Maria. *[I found the long section boring and not revealing much of interest.]*

13. Zoe, Sunday night cont'd. Her mom comes downstairs and pours a drink, then says they'll make some food "for the boys."

14. Sam, Monday morning, cont'd. Backstory. He recalls how Zoe told him she hadn't drunk any alcohol, though her blood tests showed she did. Said Jack, the boy who provided the car, wouldn't drive because he was drunk. Said Gull was her best friend.

15. **25% Mark.** Zoe, Sunday night cont'd. Helps her mom prepare food, thinks about visiting Gull's grave, how she had to hide who she was in case anyone saw. Zoe asks her what they should say about Barlow, and her mom explodes: "I don't know!" Chris drives up, and Mom tells Zoe to leave it to her and say nothing. *[One could argue that the fixed goal at this moment is centered on how to keep* *their secret from Chris and Lucas, though that goal shortly ends. There is no goal for the protagonist in this novel—a fatal flaw.]*

16. Tessa. She follows Chris and Lucas into the house. Chris wants to talk to Maria privately, but she says she must tend to the snacks.

17. Zoe. Washes face and thinks about Jack Bell, a boy at school and who held the party the night of the accident and had made a pass at her. Downstairs, Chris presses for answers about the man who made a scene, but Zoe and Maria deny knowing him.

18. Tessa. Maria continues to try to ply everyone with food, to avoid talking about the incident. Chris snaps at Lucas for being rude.

19. Zoe. Chris and Zoe set the outdoor table. He questions her again: Does she know that man in the church? She says no, trying not to look guilty. Just as they're about to eat, someone pounds on the door. Chris tells Maria to go check on the baby as he goes to answer it.

20. Sam, Monday morning, cont'd. More backstory about Zoe's weeks after the accident. He'd met with Zoe and her parents, and they discussed the online bullying, her parents insisting the bad kids lured Zoe to the party. She says she drove willingly, but didn't know she was drunk.

21. Zoe, Sunday night cont'd. Zoe is alone with Lucas. He asks her if she's read the script he sent. They are awkward together. He presses her to read the whole thing.

22. **Key Scene #3 - First Pinch Point (30%).** Tessa. Tom Barlow is at the door. He demands that Zoe pay for what she did. Chris questions him, then pushes him back. Tessa intercedes and asks Barlow if he would talk to her. He gets tearful, and she leads him away outside. She tells Chris to go back inside, notices Maria watching from upstairs. *[This would work as the pinch point if, indeed, Barlow was the opposition or played a larger opposing role in the story. He doesn't.]*

23. Zoe. Zoe and Lucas talk. Lucas wonders if she'd ever stop playing piano, and that upsets her. She wonders if he is thinking that. Then she spills food and they laugh. Chris comes in, angry. Accuses Zoe of acting like a slut. Zoe is shocked and freaked by his words and tone.

24. Tessa. She sits outside with Barlow. He recognizes her from court. Shows her the flyer he got at his door for the concert. He too had moved his family here to get away from the past. He asks Tessa if Chris knows the truth. He gestures at the fancy house and says he himself has nothing. That Zoe is a murderer and should pay. "People need to know, and I'm going to make sure they do." He walks off. Tessa follows.

25. Zoe. Tells her mom Chris wants to talk to her. Mom is on the bed playing with Grace, asks Zoe to lie down with them, giving Zoe a rare moment of closeness with her.

26. Tessa. Follows Barlow and sees he only lives a few miles away. She sees him get out, his wife ask him what's wrong, and Barlow not telling. She decides not to pursue talking to him because clearly his wife doesn't know what he just did.

27. Zoe. Chris comes upstairs. Maria leaves to talk with him. Thinks how her dad blames her mom—for pushing Zoe too hard with the music. Now they hardly talk. Her mom used to cry every night after Zoe got out of the Unit, until she met Chris.

28. Tessa. Returns Richard's call. He's drunk, as usual, but she still loves him. He wonders why she doesn't leave him. So does Sam. She says she'll be back later and rings off.

29. **Key Scene #4 - Twist #1.** Zoe. With Grace. Lucas summons her, then kisses her in the hallway. He tells her **he knows her secret, all about her.** He says they can't leave their parents alone, that "Dad can be mean sometimes." They go in kitchen, where Chris attacks Maria for not being honest. She suggests they all sit and talk, and he says it's a bit late for that. Zoe's shocked—her mom is losing it. Chris demands Lucas get out. Zoe screams. Everything has suddenly come to an explosive head. *[While this is a new*

development, it doesn't really impact the overall plot. It's more like "so what?"]

30. Tessa. Arrives at the house and hears a scream. She comes in, takes Zoe upstairs, aware that something's been revealed that has caused huge conflict. She puts Zoe on her bed, then goes downstairs.

31. Zoe. She knows she shouldn't have screamed. She thinks about being in the Unit, about Jack Bell giving her a big Coke at the party that tasted funny, then trying to seduce her. Gull had shown up, then vomited. The other girls made fun of them. Jack offered to drive Gull home. She remembers them getting in the car. Then remembers Lucas saying he *knows*. She gets her phone to read the rest of his script, not wanting to go downstairs.

32. Sam, Monday morning, cont'd. Backstory continues. Recalls how he discussed pleas with Zoe and her parents after the accident. Zoe insists on pleading guilty. *[Note: Sam's scenes have almost no present action, so they serve to provide backstory that could be revealed in Zoe's POV. I don't see the point to them at all.]*

33. Tessa. Finds Maria, Chris, and Lucas outside by the pool. Maria seems drunk, says she told Chris everything. Maria starts to undress, to Chris's horror. Maria jumps in the pool and Lucas fishes her out. Chris gets her a towel and takes her inside, softened. Then tells Tessa she should go home.

34. Zoe. Looks at her phone app. Thinks it's Lucas who wrote "I've known all along." She remembers driving the car that fateful night and the banter between the teens. She just wanted to drive slowly and take Gull home. When she missed the turn for the lighthouse—where Jack wanted to go—she accidentally hit the gas instead of the brake, and Jack swung the wheel. Tessa disrupts her reminiscing, saying Zoe's mom fell in the pool and that Tessa is heading home. Her aunt reassures her that things will be fine and Zoe paid the price for her mistake and now deserves a life.

35. Sam, Monday morning cont'd. Backstory. He remembers Zoe taking the stand, Jack's sister, Eva, stating Zoe was very drunk at

the party. She lied, saying Zoe poured vodka into her own drinks. Then another girl corroborated the testimony.

36. Tessa. Dreads going home to drunk Richard. She finds him asleep, helps him to the bathroom to pee so he won't have an accident, then cleans up the mess in the kitchen. She gets sad thinking about her marriage, about Barlow, then calls Sam.

37. Zoe. Lucas comes to get Zoe. They're to have a family talk. They go into Chris's study, where he pulls up a photo from the concert—Lucas is staring at Barlow as he and Zoe sit at the piano. Maria comes in and gasps.

38. Sam. Backstory. Tells of Zoe's sentencing. Two years later he ran into Tessa. He now watches her drive away to see Zoe after learning of Maria's death *[finally getting back to the present action for one paragraph]*.

39. Zoe. Her mom tells Chris and Lucas the whole story. Chris says he is glad she told him but upset she lied. Maria is wholly repentant. Zoe says she'll go clean up the dinner.

40. Tessa. Antsy, she heads to Sam's, though she can't reach him on the phone. Then realizes she left her phone at home. Arrives at Sam's place.

41. Zoe. She's cleaning up. Talks to Lucas about how he knew her secret. He remembered her from a piano competition years ago. Finishes and goes upstairs to be with Grace. Lies with her on the bed, notices the clock. It's midnight.

42. Tessa. Watches a movie with Sam, then they go to bed. She cries a bit before falling asleep.

43. **Key Scene #5 – Midpoint (exactly 50%).** Zoe. Wakes. Hears screaming. Runs downstairs, the front door's open. By the trash shed stand Chris, Katya, and her boyfriend. Zoe hurries over to see her mom on the ground inside, bloody and lifeless. Medics arrive. *[It's odd to have a murder/death be the Midpoint, but it is a dramatic event that now changes everything in Zoe's life.]*

44. *Zoe.* The police are there with the four teens, Chris, and the baby. Chris tells the police he'd been asleep and didn't know if Maria had been drinking. Chris accuses Barlow. The police ask them all, except Katya's boyfriend (whose father picks him up) to come down to the station. Grace worries if she will be killed next and if they'll think she killed her mom. *[I wonder why the boyfriend, who would be a main suspect, was allowed to leave, never questioned.]*

45. Tessa. Arrives at the house to see Maria carried off in a body bag. Police tell her there'll be an autopsy, and a murder inquiry has been launched.

46. Zoe. At the police station she talks to her uncle Richard. She says she wants to go with him to find Sam at his office, where they're told he's on his way. He arrives and Zoe sits down with him to tell him what happened.

47. Sam. He sits with Zoe and Richard—he sees Tessa's husband for the first time. Richard is worried; he doesn't know where Tessa is, and Sam certainly isn't going to tell him. Sam asks Zoe why she's here. She says she's scared Barlow may come after her, that she might be blamed. Sam knows he can't help her. He will possibly be a witness, and his relationship with Tessa is bound to come out.

48. Zoe. Sam calls Zoe's dad to get her. She's upset. Richard's phone rings; it's Tessa, and Richard is hysterical that she's okay. Zoe speaks with Tessa and tells her what happened. Tessa assures her she'll be cared for. Zoe and Richard head back to the police station.

49. Tessa. She's meets up with Richard and Zoe at the station. Chris is yelling. He doesn't want his family incarcerated there. Tessa offers for them to all go to her house. Once there, she goes upstairs and takes a shower and cries.

50. Zoe. Everyone's adjusting at Tessa's house. Chris talks to Zoe and assures her they're still a family. Zoe tells Lucas what torment they're in for with the investigation. He asks her to delete his script. She says no but gives in. The police arrive to question everyone separately.

51. Richard *[first time in his POV - awkward structure to add him so late in the story]*. He's thinking about all these people in the house, changing the baby's diaper, wanting a drink. Feeds the baby and determines to question Tessa later about where she was last night.

52. Sam. He's dealing with a medical issue. Meets with friend Nick George, who works in the Criminal Investigation Dept., to get info on the crime scene. They talk about his illness in vague terms, but it sounds serious.

53. Tessa. She and Richard talk a bit before the police arrive. He wants to know where she was last night, but she gives a vague answer. Police start with Chris in a private room. They ask for Zoe, but she wants Sam with her. Tessa tells her she doesn't need him. Chris scolds Zoe and tells her to cooperate. Zoe goes in.

54. Zoe. She's familiar with and wary of police interviews. They ask her friendly questions, to which she answers "no comment." They stop, and her father enters the room.

55. Tessa. Uneasy with Philip there. She hasn't seen him in years. He looks old, and she's mad he abandoned Maria. Zoe clings to him and says, "I was asleep." Tessa doesn't think Philip will be much help.

56. Sam. He's in the hospital waiting room. Nick calls, says there was blood splatter found in the house. He goes in for his test.

57. **[Pinch Point #2 should fall about here, but there is none.]** Tessa. The police question her. She tells about the night's events. They ask for her phone, which has her texts with Sam. Police tells her Barlow had a solid alibi.

58. Zoe. She sits with her dad. They argue as he defends Barlow. She pounds on him, and he doesn't know what to do.

59. Richard. Feeds the baby, chats with Lucas about movies. Zoe is led in and upstairs, and Richard notes Chris's harsh expression as he watches.

60. Zoe. She's in a room, crying. Gets on Richard's computer and downloads the rest of Lucas's script, which reveals Chris *kind of* battered Lucas's mother. *[I personally find the script inserts boring and unnecessary. Lucas could just tell Zoe his secrets.]*

61. Zoe. Stops reading. The liaison officer comes in, asks what she is looking at. Zoe lies.

62. Tessa. The police interview her, then stop because they have to attend to something. She talks to Philip, he's at a loss what to do with Zoe, Tessa slaps him, tells him to be a father. Chris takes the baby, and Tessa wonders what will become of Zoe.

63. Sam. Getting an MRI and wondering who killed Maria.

64. Zoe. Talks with Dad, who won't give her an answer about taking her. Borrows his phone and goes into the bathroom to read the rest of Lucas's script. It finishes the story of how Lucas's dying mother killed herself.

65. Richard. The police ask everyone to take a DNA test. Richard watches their resistance.

66. Tessa. In kitchen talking with Richard about Grace and Zoe. Richard starts to press redial to call Sam after Tessa told him she'd tried to reach Zoe's solicitor. Tessa freaks because she had called Sam's private number. *[This subplot between Tessa and Sam goes nowhere.]*

67. Zoe. Wonders if Chris is somehow responsible for his former wife's death. His past violence scares her. Chris wants to call a hotel and take the family there to stay. Zoe doesn't want to go, worried to have Chris take Grace.

68. Richard. He talks with Tess about Chris; she suggests he must have killed Maria. Richard presses her about Sam, about where she was last night. He worries where all this will lead.

69. Zoe. Gives Grace a bath. Lucas comes in. Zoe tells Lucas she read the script. She asks him if Chris killed his mom; he says Chris may

have made her take her life. Zoe asks if Lucas thinks Chris killed Maria.

70. Tessa. Gets Sam on the phone. He tells her they're all being investigated and blood was found in the house. She feels abandoned when Sam says he has an appointment.

71. **Key Scene #7 - Twist #2.** Zoe. She questions Lucas: Did Chris ever hurt him? The answer seems yes. But Lucas does not think Chris killed Maria. **Lucas suddenly admits he killed Maria,** trying to protect her. *[This admission is awkwardly plopped into the story at an odd spot, and Zoe hardly reacts to Lucas's killing her mom.]*

72. Sam. He sits with doctor, waiting for the results of the MRI. *[A lot of build for this minor character we don't really care about. A subplot that doesn't go anywhere.]*

73. **Key Scene #8 – Dark Night.** Zoe. Lucas explains that, in protecting her mother from Chris, he knocked her down the stairs *[which no one else in the house heard?]*. Lucas leaves the room. Zoe's dad comes in, and she tells him she doesn't want Grace to be around Chris. *[She doesn't think to tell anyone that Lucas killed her mom??]* She finds Lucas and asks him to come with her and she kisses his fingers. *[Okay, really lost me there. Affection for the person who killed her mother? This should be a dark moment for Zoe, but she's hardly disturbed by the truth.]*

74. Tessa. The taxi arrives to take the family to a hotel. Chris calls for Lucas, but he doesn't answer. Tessa spots Zoe and Lucas with baby in the garden. Chris agrees to go and come back later for them once he's settled in.

75. Zoe. Lucas tells details of Maria's death, and how Chris made him clean up the blood while Chris took the body to the trash shed. Chris told him to say they were both asleep when Maria died. Zoe has a plan so she can keep Grace with her and away from Chris.

76. Sam. Doctor thinks Sam has MS. Sam heads home.

77. Zoe. She tells Lucas what he should do—lie and say Chris killed Maria. He resists, but she persuades him. He recorded the argument between Chris and Maria right before she died.

78. Richard. Chris asks to use Richard's computer. *[Why don't the police quickly learn Tessa had been sleeping with Sam? They would consider Richard a possible suspect as well and take his phone and computer.]* He's tempted to drink but abstains.

79. Tessa. Zoe gets everyone to come into the sitting room. Lucas is going to show them the recording from last night.

80. **Key Scene #9 – Big Climax.** Lucas. Everyone watches how Chris went after Maria, threatening her. The camera falls, so all they can do is listen to the part where she tumbles down the stairs. Zoe then says she came out of her room and saw Chris push Maria. The police take Chris, and Zoe's dad rushes out and leaves. *[Another big flaw is that this is the only scene in Lucas's POV—not good structure. The big climax should be in the protagonist's POV.]*

81. Sam. He's having a beer, thinking what a bad future lies ahead. His cop friend tells him there's been an arrest. Sam sees a grainy photo that looks like Chris in a police car.

82. Tessa. She and Richard talk briefly about Zoe; he cries. The phone rings.

83. Richard. Determined to sober up and take custody of the kids. He thought he'd heard Lucas earlier saying "It was an accident."

84. Sam. He and Richard talk. Richard suspects Tessa was with him. He tells Sam to leave them alone, then hangs up. He doesn't know what to do with his life. *[But who cares? He's not at all important in this plot.]*

85. **Key Scene #10 – Resolution.** Epilogue. Zoe. Six months later. Zoe is again performing a concert. The kids have been living with Tessa and Richard. Chris is in prison. She plays the piece in memory of her mother.

What We Learn from This

So, here we have a very weak premise, a barely empathetic protagonist without a goal, characters who often behave unbelievably, and little plot. After Maria is discovered dead, there is little emotional reaction. No one (including the police) seems to be concerned over how Maria died and if the killer is at large or among them.

There is no tension built in a lengthy investigation. The "big" elements of the story are Lucas revealing Chris has a little bit of a violent nature, which we don't see, and that because of Chris's secretive violence, Lucas felt compelled to protect Maria from Chris. Most of the novel is narrative, backstory, or characters thinking.

I hope you can see how the subplot of Sam having a medical issue is no subplot at all. As you've learned in this book, subplots not only need to be well developed and have an arc, they have to impact the protagonist and her efforts to reach her goal. In this novel, there is no goal. The death comes at the midpoint, which makes little sense, and while one could guess Zoe's goal would be to uncover who killed her mother, she doesn't make any attempt to do so, and the thought barely crosses her mind.

Because there is no fixed goal, there is no build to the climax, where the goal is either reached or not. Somewhere along the way, Zoe starts feeling protective of Grace and caring about her (whereas she hasn't up till that point), and she decides her goal is to protect Grace by colluding with Lucas to pin the murder on Chris.

Which makes her more unlikable. We don't feel she is doing this for any honorable reason—because we never really believe she or Maria was in danger from Chris. She wants to spare Lucas from jail too, but that's not a strong motivation for her. If Chris is the opposition, then the "force" of his power should be shown in the pinch points. Make sense? That would make for a tense drama—this subtle face-off that could grow between Zoe and her stepfather. But it's not there.

There is a clear climax, with Lucas framing his father and Zoe colluding. But it's done quickly, and there is no real satisfaction in it for the reader, in my opinion.

If you look carefully, there are key places where important reaction scenes are missing. Characters should react after Maria is found murdered. Zoe should react to Lucas's admission of killing her mother.

Structurally, this novel is flawed throughout. So here's your assignment . . .

* * *

Your assignment: Here's a big challenge. How would you restructure this flawed novel so that it has strong structure? Start with identifying Zoe's goal for the novel and work backward to a setup, Inciting Incident, a key scene at around 25% that locks in Zoe's goal, big twists or complications, clear opposition, and effective pinch points. If the end result is that Zoe colludes with Lucas and "gets away with murder," whereas she didn't get off in the accident, think about how this ties in with the goal.

Ultimately, this novel needs a great premise and a powerful theme (and a better, more relative title). I can imagine some of the possible themes—can you? Themes are best driven home in the Midpoint, Dark Night moment, and the Climax scene. Use the Ten Key Scene Chart to lay out those scenes.

I hope this experiment helps you see how layering with those foundational scenes makes for a solid story.

Chapter 18: Another Structurally Flawed Novel

Kenneth Johnson's 2017 supernatural best seller *The Man of Legends* blends adventure, romance, and drama to create a uniquely styled novel that doesn't adhere to the usual conventions. This story that consists of multiple first-person POVs has a large cast, though many of the scenes in POV seem wholly unnecessary and blah.

Johnson sets up tension for an event about to occur by introducing the cast as they either interact with the protagonist, Will, or talk about him. It's clear from the start that Will is not an ordinary human. And he knows suspects something catastrophic is about to happen—but that never pans out.

This story is a blend of elements seen in *Dr. Who, 12 Monkeys, Groundhog Day*, and *Star Trek* episodes, and its strength lies in the unique voices of each character (though at times the speed at which the author flips from one to another is too much and disrupts my concentration).

I feel the novel has some serious structural flaws. There's a nice build of tension as things develop and as Will's past is revealed. But the book is mostly backstory and narrative, which slows the pacing and probably loses some readers—especially those hoping for a fast-paced thriller. There is little real action to speak of, and part of the problem lies in this novel set up as a collection of testimonials from various people who intersected with Will during those few days.

To be honest, I gave up analyzing this book about three-quarters in, deciding to ditch it due to my frustration with the weak structure. But I picked it up again and slogged through the last chapters in order to finish my task.

Overall, I feel the novel fails because it's lacking the ten key scenes in the proper places. Maybe that sounds simplistic, but I believe any good teacher of story structure would say the same thing.

Let's take a look at the summary of scenes, and, again, I'll note what scenes I can in an attempt to identify if and where any of the ten key scenes are placed. I hope that you'll spot the flaws in this structure, particularly in the absence of a clear, strong Midpoint scene and Dark Night moment. Because there really isn't a goal for the protagonist, the entire framework of this story collapses.

Take a look and see what you think.

The POV character is noted at the start of each scene summary, and the POV shifts are also noted in italics.

The Man of Legends
By Kenneth Johnson

1. **Key Scene #1 – Setup.** *Will, 33.* The novel starts just before New Year's of 2001 with a dream sequence in which Will is moving through different times. First, he's a monk in 13th century Paris, being chased into a cathedral. Then he's in a 19th century Western saloon in Nevada. From there he becomes a 1930s gangster in Chicago, where he's shot. Bleeding, he opens a manhole and falls onto a cart of Plague victims. Priests are after him—the Pope wants him—as he's engulfed in flames. When Will shakes awake, he's in his present day on a NY subway. Though he feels his life has "much positive promise," he senses something disturbing in the subway tunnel as he heads home. We get the feeling that wasn't just a dream and Will is not an ordinary man.

2. *Jillian Guthrie,* journalist. Brief scene. Christmas. She's heading somewhere and bumps into a man, which jiggles a memory of when she was five and crashed into a similar man on her bike. Hurries on. *[This scene ties in with backstory near the end but doesn't serve any helpful purpose in the novel.]*

3. *Will.* As he walks to Columbia U, a cop watches him. He tries to "act normal." He sees a toddler who speaks to him in a dark male voice: "You oughta just give it the hell up, man." Memories of other time periods keep popping up.

4. *Eleanor Edgerton,* 61, vagrant. Sees Will walk by and notices a blind man actually sees him. The a statue in the park turns its head as Will walks by. Will asks her to come with him. He takes her to a church and tells a man there to examine her. "She's diabetic," Will says. She wonders how he knows that. *Will's POV*: It worries him that "dark and potent forces" are escalating their effort. He starts to head in one direction, but it makes him suddenly ill. Realizing his mistake, he adjusts course and feels immediately better.

5. *Chuck Weston*, 52, singer. Will chats him up about his gigs and guitar, indicating he's a huge fan. Chuck lets Will play his precious guitar and is amazed at the guy's talent. Chuck's been down and out and drinking hard, but Will tells he needs to be real, get back to his roots, stop drinking. As hinted at before, he mentions that something is about to happen in a couple of days. We begin to see a pattern of Will seeming to care about the disenfranchised and that it's part of some bigger plan on Will's part. Chuck ends with saying he didn't see Will again until the disaster at the warehouse.

6. *Will.* Brief paragraph showing how much he enjoyed playing the guitar. *Nicole Jackson,* student, 23. She's tending bar, and Will's there. He notices she's been crying. She had a dream about her recently deceased dog. Like the others we've seen so far, she too feels strangely compelled to open up and talk to Will, to trust him. We get that Will has outlived those he's loved. Again, Will makes reference to something that is about to happen. A couple walks in discussing Pascal. *Will's POV*. He quotes Pascal in French without thinking. He considers an attractive woman in the bar, then Nicole turns into a man speaking "the ancient language" and tempting him. "How about it?" the man says. Will curses him. *Nicole's POV*. She's stunned at Will's strange outburst. The other woman asks what language he spoke. Will says Aramaic. He tips Nicole and tells her there are puppies at the pound about to be put down. She ends with, "I didn't see him again until five days later—when we

were trapped together inside the warehouse. That unbelievable nightmare. Not everyone got out alive."

7. *Jillian.* On subway thinking about her career, foreshadowing meeting Will. She arrives at work, a sensationalist rag, and banters with her boss and coworkers. When she pulls out a photo of Ghandi from the 1940s, she notices a man standing behind him (who is clearly Will, in his thirties) but at that moment doesn't know who he is.

8. *Tito Brown*, 17, tagger. He's spraying a wall, when Will comes up and talks to him. As always, Will connects quickly and earns trust, gives him advice. *Will's POV.* His phone rings. An art gallery owner tells Will he sold one of his paintings to a woman who wants to meet him. When Will says no, he learns her name— Hanna, an elderly woman he knows well. Implied he'd been close to her at one time. We already get that he doesn't age. He tells Tito to meet him in two days on E. 126th but doesn't say why. He thinks *Hanna . . .*

9. **Key Scene #2 - Inciting Incident (11% mark).** *Hanna Claire*, 85. She's in her home and Father Paul arrives. He's come to look at a painting she has. She's thinking about Will. Learns the priest just came all the way from Rome. *Father Paul's POV.* He tries to hold his surprise and anxiety upon learning Hanna had known the artist. He's clearly on a mission. She tells how she met Will in 1937 when he saved her from drowning—a suicide attempt when she was young and he was in his thirties. *Hanna's POV.* The priest plies her with questions about Will: has she seen him, when last, where to find him. He gives her the excuse that someone he knows wants to commission Will to do a painting. She calls him Will's arch-nemesis, then pulls out a Bible to get him to promise that if he finds Will, he will not hurt him. *Priest's POV.* We learn he's been searching for Will for twenty-three years and will lie if he has to. She shows him another painting by Will, and they talk about a similar one in the Met dated 1883, signed the same. She promises to tell the priest if she finds Will; he promises the same to her. But it is an uneasy agreement. *[I note this as the inciting incident because it's Hanna finding Will, and, hence, Father Paul learning Hanna*

has found him, that sets the story rolling. Up until now, Will has been living day to day. But now, things change, and the stakes ramp into high gear.]

10. *Minos Volonikis*, 24, student at Columbia. He's just arrived from Greece—hungry and cold. The airlines lost his suitcase. He walks by Will, who is taking photos and tells him *in Greek* to eat his sandwich. They talk and Will offers him money. *Will's POV*. An editor at his publisher's, Laura, calls to tell him his latest history book's art cover is ready and gushes about his talent to capture events "as if you were in the room." We learn he's a prolifically published history author and that his emphasis is on promoting morality and ethical treatment of others. *Laura's POV*. She presses him to do appearances; he's in high demand. But he declines, showing a kind interest in her writing. Then she hears his hesitation when she mentions a priest from Rome asked about him.

11. *Father Paul.* On the subway, he recalls meeting the Pope in 1977. A strange meeting, indicating Paul had been chosen for something. An archbishop had given him a combination to a safe and told him to read the journal he would find in there. "We nearly trapped the bastard," he's told. Now it's up to Paul. At SoHo, he goes to the gallery and looks at Will's paintings. When asked, the gallery owner, Walter, tells the priest he has no contact info for Will. Shows interest in the paintings, asks to see some letters in Will's handwriting, out of curiosity. He recognizes the handwriting and snaps pictures with a hidden camera. Asks Walter to call Will to see if he would do a commission, though the gallery owner says it's unlikely. However, the priest memorizes the phone number Walter dials in front of him, recognizing the Philadelphia area code.

12. *Renji*, 43, Rastafarian busker. Talking religion with a friend while smoking weed. Will walks by. *Will's POV*. He's talking on the phone to Walter, hands the black men some money and tells them to buy iron tablets. Alarmed to learn a priest was at the gallery, he tells Walter to tell the man nothing. Then one of the black men turns into the young man he'd seen in the bar and warns Will: "You'll never buy your way out, pal." He "turns back" into the old vagrant. As Will leaves, he calls back in Latin: "You're getting

nervous, huh? Only one day to go?" But the young man doesn't reappear. *Father Paul's POV*. He enters his hotel, then calls a young priest in Rome, then asks if he received the email, which has the handwriting sample. The young priest says he'll begin the analysis right away. Paul feels anxious over what is about to happen and wonders if Will does also.

13. *Tito*. New Year's Eve, he heads to Will's motor home parked on the street, knocks, hears Will playing a violin. They talk. *Will's POV*. Will gives him a bag of paints and a sketchbook, encourages him to go to art school. Tito tells Will about his hard life and asks why he's helping. Will says, "I like to invest in possibilities."

14. *Jillian*. She shuffles through photos and see one of Teddy Roosevelt. Will is in the background (though she doesn't know who he is yet). *Tito's POV*. He goes into the Met Museum, astonished at the art. *Father Paul's POV*. He's waiting to meet with an archbishop. Goes to the Met to meet with an expert, who shows him a painting that he suspects Will painted. *Tito's POV*. Hears the priest talk with the expert, follows, listens. The priest wants to know if there are more paintings by this artist.

15. **25% Mark – Goal Fixed.** *Jillian*. She and coworker Steve compare the Ghandi photo with the Roosevelt one (38 years apart). Will looks the same age in both. Jillian adds a third photo from the Civil War. She is now convinced this is the same man, and she must find out who he is . . . and find him. *[Though Will is the protagonist, Jillian's story follows the traditional structure of goal fixed at this juncture, then pursuit of goal continues, with resolution at the climax. However, Will has no goal for the novel other than the one he's had for years.]* *Tito's POV*. He follows priest and expert to another painting that is signed J.W. instead of W. J. It's a self-portrait dated 1677. Tito is stunned. It's an exact likeness of Will, and the man is wearing the necklace Will wears.

16. *Suki Tamura, 42, taxi driver*. Recounts New Year's Eve, when her cab window was shot out, a robber demanding her money. Just then a man grabbed the punk, threatened him, and said "I'll be watching you." Her "savior" speaks to her in Japanese, asks if she's okay. She notes: "I didn't see him until three days later . . .

on that really scary day." *Father Paul's POV*. Goes to archdiocese to meet with Cardinal Malloy. Paul is annoyed the cardinal hasn't done what he's asked—to get the NYPD to trace that call from the gallery. Malloy demands to know what Paul is up to. *Jillian's POV*. Verifies the photos are authentic. *Father Paul's POV*. Malloy looks at the photo of Will's letter, learns there are matching samples of his handwriting across 1,600 years. Malloy is rattled: "What exactly are we dealing with?"

17. *Jillian*. In apartment on New Year's Eve watching TV, missing her office party, missing her dead mother. *Father Paul's POV*. Tries to get the NYPD to help him track Will. They agree to pick him up in the morning to use GPS to locate him. The priest can't wait to reveal the truth about Will to the world. He's very ambitious and power-hungry. *Tito's POV*. Fretting over Will looking exactly like that painting. *Hanna's POV*. Mourning over her lost life with Will. *Will's POV*. He's in a church, hoping the new millennium will usher in his long-awaited hopes. Release from his "curse." But as the minister is preaching about Jesus's crucifixion and celebrations erupt in Times Square, nothing happens.

18. *Will*. Tries to be hopeful, then candles blow out and a dark voice tells him that maybe Jesus won't show at all. Sees the young man from before and says, "It's not over, you bastard." He wanders the city all night, getting depressed, begging, "Please, reveal yourself."

19. **Key Scene #3 - First Pinch Point (33%)**. *Father Paul*. Police pick him up, as they drive, they snag Will's location via GPS. He presses the cops. He has to catch him. The man is guilty of murder! *[We've seen up till now the priest searching for Will, as he's been doing for years. But it's only now that he has actually located him, in this city, and he is bringing all his force to bear on finding him.]* *Will's POV*. Heading to the subway in a foul mood. *Father Paul's POV*. They lose Will's signal. Paul is furious. Cops suggest he may have gone down into the subway. *Will's POV*. While waiting on the subway platform, a crazed man threatens to jump. Will, at his patience's end, grabs the man and suggests they jump together. The man freaks and runs. People around Will speak to him in Russian, warning him (they aren't aware someone is speaking through them). Will, raging, enters the subway car. *Father Paul's POV*. He

dashes with cops down to the subway, searching frantically but doesn't see Will. Cop says he may have gotten on the last train. They'll head to 103rd Street and see if they can pick up the signal again.

20. *Will.* In subway, gets claustrophobic, stumbles off at some stop and heads up to the street. *Father Paul's POV.* In car, cops put out an APB for Will, then catch his signal in Spanish Harlem. *Will's POV.* Nightmare memories assail him. Different people are used to speak to him. "He ain't coming" and "But I'm right here for you, Will." He stumbles on. *Father Paul's POV.* Still in pursuit. *Will's POV.* Heads NE toward his motor home. At 112th, he sees a tenement house on fire. On the fourth floor, a woman screams. Her child is trapped. Will tries to ignore, but can't. "No, I don't want to do this anymore!" But then he runs inside. *Father Paul's POV.* Homes in on 112th Street, two blocks ahead. *Will's POV.* Runs through flames and smoke to the second floor, hears the child crying. *Father Paul's POV.* Stops and watches the firemen work, searches the crowd. Will has to be here! *Will's POV.* He finds the child, flames all around. He tosses her down to firefighters three floors below. He faints in pain. *Father Paul's POV.* Sees the firefighters with the child, then a body is hauled out of the building. He sees it is Will! His legs are broken and he's badly burnt; doesn't look like he'll survive. As the ambulance races off, Paul and cops are right behind.

21. **Key Scene #4 - Twist #1.** *Will.* His mind floats in a coma. Recalls his early days in the first century, traveled, lived in monasteries, tried to learn why he never aged or died. In 760 he tries to assure crowds a comet isn't going to destroy them. He's beaten to death.

22. *Dr. Fernandez, 44, trauma specialist.* Treats Will, who is in coma in Emergency. *Hanna's POV.* Sees the news of the fire on TV, sees Will's face on the body dragged out. Shocked. *Jillian's POV.* Steve grabs Jillian. They see Will on TV, head to the hospital. *Will's POV.* More drifting through memories *[author is using this as a device to fill in a lot of backstory of Will's many experiences]*. This memory is how he met Ghandi, the Vatican after Will, he escapes on board a ship.

23. *Jillian.* She goes into the hospital with Chris, a photographer. Sees the priest as they hurry by the ICU. *Father Paul's POV.* He watches the news people run to room 304 and follows. *Jillian's POV.* Will is comatose; Chris takes photos. The priest comes in. Dr. kicks them out. Jillian sees an old woman rushing to Will's room and wonders if the woman can ID him. *Hanna's POV.* She's shocked: it is Will! *Jillian's POV.* Follows the old woman, hears her speak to the nurse. She tells nurse she's a good friend and his name is W. J. Jillian questions Hanna, but the old woman will say no more. *Hanna's POV.* See that Father Paul is there, startles her. *Jillian's POV.* She calls Steve. Says he is the guy but doesn't know his name yet. Tells him to research Hanna Claire. She's the key.

24. *Will.* Has more memories, these of chatting with a young German in 1904 about theoretical physics (Einstein). *Jillian's POV.* At night, she is still in the hospital waiting room, as is the priest. Nurse tries to wake Will.

25. *Will.* Hears the nurse's voice. Still lost in the past, with Melville, who wrote *Moby Dick.*

26. *Father Paul.* He's waiting to see if Will wakens. *Will's POV.* Memories now of 1930s Chicago gangsters. Then recalls his anticipation and letdown at the arrival of the year 1000, where he had hoped for release or answers then too. *Tito's POV.* Knocking at the motor home, looking for Will. *Jillian's POV.* Chris comes to the hospital. The mother and girl who were saved in the fire show up. The girl goes in to thank Will. *Maria Encalada, 5.* Sees Will, thanks him, prays for him. *Jillian's POV.* Watches the girl come out of the room.

27. *Will.* Hears a child's voice. Remembers being with Kepler and discussing astronomy. He confides in Percy and Mary Shelley, who comfort him.

28. *Maria.* They leave the hospital, and she hears mean remarks about her druggie mom. *Will's POV.* Recalls seeing doctors over the centuries, trying to get answers to his condition, feeling hopeless to change his life's course. *Jillian's POV.* A nurse tells her Will is improving. Says the firefighters found his wallet and ID. *Will's*

POV. He starts to feel pain. *Father Paul's POV.* Hears a sound from Will's room and sees he is waking. *Jillian's POV.* She takes a cab to the known address of J. W. Aldritch at 177th Street. Steve calls her and says Aldritch died seven years ago, and he can't find anything useful on Hanna.

29. *Will.* Still floundering in memories. *[To me, this goes on way too long.]* *Father Paul's POV.* Angry that the cardinal isn't heeding Paul's directives and authority. See's Will is moving. *Maria.* She's been taken to an "uncle's" place. She overhears adults talking about using her as a mule to carry drugs. *Father Paul's POV.* Will is waking. Paul plans to take him to the Vatican with help of the NYPD. *Will's POV.* He's remembering how he made Levi Strauss famous back in SF in the 1800s.

30. **Key Scene #5 – Midpoint (50% mark).** *Will.* Recalls being in the burning building, reminding him of watching heretics burn at the stake. *Maria's POV.* She's drawing pictures of the fire. Her "uncle" touches her. *Will's POV.* He relives the pain of the fire, and the young man says in Latin, "I know you can hear me." *Father Paul's POV.* Overhears the "nurse" speaking the words in Latin, in a male voice. Then hears Will moan and say, "Leave me be . . . Asmodeus." Father Paul freezes. The nurse comes out of the room. Paul asks her why she spoke in Latin, but she reacts puzzled. The reporter comes in. Will mutters again, "Asmodeus." *Jillian's POV.* Pushes past the priest and goes to Will's bedside. *[While this is the Midpoint, having him partially wake doesn't fit the Midpoint moment at all. There is no big realization or deeper commitment to the goal—no goal. All that happens for chapters, at this point, is Will is remembering his past and slowly waking and telling some of his story to Jillian and the priest.]*

31. *Jillian.* She and the priest try to talk to Will, who is only partially conscious. He is speaking in Latin. The priest tells her those are names for Satan he's saying. *Will's POV.* Slips back into memories of the 1600s, Lord Bacon, others. *Jillian's POV.* Learns Will is recovering amazingly. They've given Will Pentothal, which is making him tell the truth. She finally gets Will to answer questions. Gives many names, and says he's from Judea. *Will's POV.* He envisions Judea, and speaks in Latin to her. *Jillian's POV.* Asks if he

can speak English. Then he does, telling her he'd lived in Judea for thirty-three years, over two thousand years ago. The priest is amazed and speechless. She asks, "How is this possible?" Will mentions a curse he got "three days after *he* was killed" (he, meaning Jesus). Then complains of the pain. *Will's POV.* Recalls the pain back then, stumbling around Judea, seeing that young man. Each time he went in one direction, toward home, the pain would strike. When he went in an opposite direction, the pain vanished. *Jillian's POV.* Will tells her how he sought refuge with a leather merchant named Livia, whom he married and had a son with. *Will's POV.* After he recovered, he tried to go home but still couldn't. Then the pain returned, and he had to go three thousand feet away to relieve the pain. He realized he could not stay in one place more than three days. He was forced to wander. *Father Paul's POV.* Asks Will: "Why three days, three thousand feet?" but Will doesn't know. Then tells how he was trampled to death by a chariot. *Will's POV.* Recalls dying, but he recovered fully—a miracle.

32. *Jillian.* Thinks it odd the priest is not surprised by Will's story. *Will's POV.* Continues recalling those first days, trying to get help, understanding. Seeing that young man from time to time. *Jillian's POV.* Listening to Will's story. Hearing how he had to keep moving, watching his family age as he stayed the same. *Will's POV.* Years later his family comes to see him in Petra. His wife is dying and his children are old. *Jillian's POV.* Listens as Will tells how he watched his wife die and now knew what he had to do. *Will's POV.* After saying good-bye to his old children, he hurled himself off a cliff to die. *Father Paul's POV.* Listens as Will tells how he didn't die, merely suffered horrible pain. *[The continual interruption of story by shifting POVs is also very annoying to me, as a reader. And this is a lot of "telling" and backstory.]* *Will's POV.* Tells how he recovered and hid in a cave, pleading the gods for help. *Jillian's POV.* Will keeps recounting, at the urging of the priest, saying how he wandered the world for centuries. He learned he could return to a place after 333 years, so he went back to the site of the crucifixion. The priest is shocked Will witnessed Jesus's death. Will says that was the day of his crime, but says no more. The priest walks out of the room, and Jillian calls Steve, then Hanna Claire.

33. *Hanna.* Jillian calls and tells her some of what Will said, wanting her response, but Hanna pretends confusion. *Jillian's POV.* She assures Hanna she means well and won't share this story unless Hanna or Will want her to. *Hanna's POV.* She agrees to come and talk to Jillian, then warns her not to talk to the priest. *Will's POV.* He continues with his story, often seeing the young man through the centuries. *Jillian* wonders if that man is also "cursed" like Will *[the POV's keep switching as he tells his story].* Will tells how he tried to die over and over. Jillian asks what his crime was. Will says he was captain of Pilate's guard and watched Jesus's crucifixion. When the whipped and beaten Christ stopped on his doorstep, under the weight of the cross he was carrying, Will had struck Jesus and told him to go away. Jesus then said to him, "I go. But thou shalt here remain . . . thou diest not . . . but walk until I come again." *Jillian's POV.* The priest gets up, scoffs, claims this is all ridiculous, but Jillian says nothing. The priest leaves.

34. **Key Scene #6 - Pinch Pont #2.** *Father Paul.* He calls his contact at the Vatican, boasts of his find and how he is about to take him captive. He fantasizes all the acclaim and promotion he will get— maybe even become Pope. *[This is the right place for this pinch point; however there isn't really any action or new info here. We are just seeing, again, how he plans to take Will to Rome.]* *Jillian.* While waiting by Will's room, she has Steve look up references to "wandering Jew," apparently named after Will. Steve tells her there are references to him in literature throughout the ages. *Maria.* Her "uncle" tries to touch her; she misses her mom. *[I don't see how these scenes with Maria, and especially in her POV, are useful.]* *Jillian.* Hanna shows up. They talk. Hanna warns Jillian about the priest. He shows up, and they move down the hall to talk privately. *Father Paul.* He's waiting for the police to come. *Jillian.* Hanna tells her whole story about Will and says the Vatican is trying to capture him. They talk about miracles and Jesus and how the stories of Jesus's powers had been exaggerated. Will tries to make Christianity an ethical way of life, not a religion.

35. *Jillian.* She and Hanna talk, worry about the priest. *Will.* He finally wakes and talks to her. They talk about many people he met over the centuries, how they missed each other. *Maria.* She escapes from the house and heads down the street at night.

36. *Father Paul.* Paces, waiting for the police, recalling some things he'd learned about Will. *Maria.* Still walking. *Will.* He and Hanna talk more. He tells her he's exhausted and wants this all to end.

37. **Key Scene #7 - Twist #2 [Will escapes—not much of a twist].** *Tito.* Sees newspaper showing Will and the fire. *Jillian.* Worrying about what the priest will do. *Father Paul.* The cardinal arrives. They chat amiably (no urgency). They enter the hospital and tell the doctor they will post police watch and then take Will when he comes to. The doctor says his condition is critical (though we've been seeing it's not). *Jillian.* When they get to Will's room, they find he's gone. Jillian runs outside and sees Hanna pushing Will in a wheelchair. She runs over, hails a cab, and they all get in and rush away. *Father Paul.* Runs outside but can't find Will. *Jillian.* They discuss where to go, and Jillian thinks it would be best for Will to speak out. But he's done this before, and because he knows the Catholic Church has not told the truth about Jesus, the church is after him, and it's not safe. They head to Harlem as Will seems to be mostly coherent now. *Will.* He wishes he could be mortal like everyone else. Passes the young man who is on the sidewalk.

38. *Maria.* Walking the street, feeling led in some direction. *Father Paul.* With the doctor looking at the CCTV footage showing Will up and walking out of the hospital. The priest shows the doctor photos of Will through the ages, explaining the situation. The doctor is suspicious of the church's motives regarding capturing Will, but he's then bribed with visions of glory, of the groundbreaking discoveries he will make while studying Will. *Tito.* Arrives at the hospital and sees the priest and cops on the street. *Jillian.* Hanna recounts so many brave selfless things Will has done, and though he wants to give up, she won't let him. *Tito.* He's riding in the car with the priest and cops. They've told him they need his help finding Will, that Will is sick. Tito directs him to Will's motor home. *Nicole [whom we have only seen one early POV scene with].* She feels compelled to get off the subway train, doesn't know why, a new puppy on her lap. *Jillian.* The driver changes into the young man Will always sees. He races full speed at a warehouse, the doors of which "magically" open for them.

39. *Tito.* Watches the priest rip apart Will's motor home. Upset, Tito feels compelled to head over to the Westside. *Jillian.* Freaked out. Hanna says, "It's him, isn't it?" to Will. Jillian wants answers. Will gets out. The warehouse is filled with furniture and theatrical items. The mysterious young man walks around, making mannequins come to life. He talks with Will. Hanna tells Jillian he's not human. Will and the man argue, but Will's opponent doesn't say what he wants.

40. *Jillian.* Seems like the man is trying to persuade Will to go over to "the dark side" and join him, assuring Will he'll be happier that way. *Will.* Realizes the young man must be Satan *[though I wonder why it's taken him 2,000 years to conclude this].* *Jillian.* The man asks Will if he'd really believed Jesus was going to release him at the millennium. Will says yes, despondent. *Will.* The "Devil" keeps trying to persuade Will to join him, assuring him he can relieve Will's curse. Hanna begs Will not to believe him. *Jillian.* Sees Hanna choke. Will rushes to help her. The Devil tells Will he merely shut her up so they can talk. *Maria.* Gets into a cab. *Suki.* The girl points in a direction. Suki feels compelled to go that way too. *Tito.* Jumps on a subway train.

41. *Jillian.* She thinks Will was tempted by the other man, but seeing Hanna gave him resolve to resist. *Will.* A long argument ensues, with Satan belittling what Will has accomplished and Hanna taking the other side. A mannequin takes Will's first wife's form. He wants Will to "join his side," but Will says no. So Satan says he'll take someone else.

42. *Chuck (and Laura, and Renji).* Each feels compelled to head toward the warehouse *[no idea who does the compelling].* *Jillian.* Will asks if Satan will let the women go if he agrees. Hanna lunges for him; Satan hurls her back. Will rushes to Hanna, who is dead. Will presses his ancient cross against her, and she comes back to life.

43. **[Should be Key Scene #8 – Dark Night. But there's no real despairing moment.].** *Jillian.* She asks Will what he did. He lets her touch the cross. She sees a vision of Will's first wife at the foot of Jesus's cross. *Tito.* Taxi stops. He and Suki and Maria all rush together up the street, then screech to a halt at what they see.

Jillian. Hanna tells Will that while she was dead, she saw a bright light and "others" telling her to say to Will he is on the right track, making them proud. She tells him there's a larger plan. Then she dies (for real this time). The door opens and Tito, Suki, and Maria walk in. Satan is pleased they've arrived. *Will.* Sees a huge crowd outside. They don't know why they've come. He recognizes many he'd helped, and some are from centuries past. *Father Paul.* A cop yells to Paul that Will's been spotted. *Jillian.* Will asks Satan what the larger plan is. *Will.* Satan demands Will come with him now. Will walks toward him, trying to figure out the plan. *Jillian.* Everyone watching seems to feel dread. *[yawn . . .]*

44. **Key Scene #9 – Big Climax.** *Will.* Senses Satan is nervous or fearful. Wonders aloud if his task is really to persuade the evil one to come over to the light. *Jillian.* The two men are speaking in Latin, and the young man howls, causing the walls and ceiling to rumble and crack. The doors lock and two big cats appear. *Various POVs.* Satan changes into a huge monster who rages at Will. *Jillian.* Will challenges him to repent. Satan is about to shatter the building. Will starts to take Satan's hand, though the crowd chants, "No!" then Satan turns into a beautiful angel of light. *Will.* Recognizes Lucifer, the angel of light, how he was before he fell. *Jillian.* Everyone is spellbound at the sight. A bright light comes down, and Lucifer is terrified. He writhes and tries to yank his hand from Will's but can't. As he rises into the light, Will hangs on. Will says something in Latin; Lucifer breaks free and turns into a massive gruesome dragon, then is sucked underground in fire. Will gets to his feet. *Will.* Moved by all the support. Tito warns him the priest is coming. *Father Paul.* He arrives, pushes through the crowd in the warehouse, demands to know where Will is, but Will has gone. *Jillian.* She sees how angry the priest is. Leaves with Maria, promising to take care of her.

45. *Father Paul.* Suffers from some ailment, prays a long prayer to God. *Jillian.* Talking from years later, saying how she collected testimonials from those in the warehouse and published a book sixteen years ago. Two weeks after the warehouse showdown, she got a letter from the priest who, dying, sent her a CD and his journal, with all the research on Will.

46. **Key Scene #10 – Resolution.** *Jillian.* Sixteen years after the warehouse incident, she's at Maria's college graduation. Will shows up and seems content, at peace. Says Satan leaves him alone now. Some days later Jillian gets a package from Will with a flash drive full of his stories. *Will.* He listens to Chuck on the radio and admires Tito's wonderful artwork. Realizes his curse is really a "grand mission" to actively seek out his enemy and keep trying to lure him into the light, thinking that will save the entire world. Gives an old man some change and thinks he might be an angel.

Similar to *The Perfect Girl*, this novel is so lacking in action. The pages are filled with backstory, characters sitting around thinking, and passages telling of all the famous people Will had encountered and influenced across time. But present action? Hardly any at all.

Will meets some people, saves a girl, ends up in the hospital. The priest finds him and waits to take him to the Pope. People gather at the hospital, then there's a kind of chase scene. The big climax is a calm discussion in a warehouse that leads to an almost comic standoff, with a crowd uselessly standing by. Boring.

Many of the characters seem like filler in the story. Why so many scenes with Maria, a five-year-old? Tito, the punk? Two scenes only with Nicole the dog lover, Chuck the musician, and Suki the cab driver. They don't serve a strong purpose in the story. And when all these minor characters gather at the climax, they don't do much else but watch and pat Will on the back for a good job done, after he defeats Satan.

So many POV sections accomplish nothing. Whatever useful points are brought out could be revealed while staying in one POV the entire chapter. It feels as if a movie camera was jerking from person to person in a kind of *Blair Witch* chaos, unable to rest more than a minute on one person. Too many scenes are in Jillian's POV, which gives the feel that this is her story . . . but it's not.

The Goal at the Crux of Great Storytelling

What's missing that would make this novel work? First off: *some setup that leads to a clear goal.* As with *The Perfect Girl*, there is no goal for the novel. While Will is tired of his curse and hoping for some escape, and there is an occasional mention of a warehouse incident, he doesn't develop a goal for the novel—a visible plot goal that locks in what this novel is about. Without a goal, there doesn't seem to be a point to the book or to Will's character. Who wants to see a guy wandering around, depressed and fed up, with no real plan?

Second: *opposition that really pinches*. While we see the opposition, again, there is very little active buildup that shows the opposition creating huge problems—and those problems should be specifically impacting the attempt at the goal. Yes, it's a cat-and-mouse game, to some extent, with the priest finding Will fairly easily. But he finds him before the Midpoint, and for most of the second half of the book just sits around waiting for the police to come and help him kidnap Will to take him to Rome. And then he arrives at the end, missing him again. Yawn.

What are the stakes? Just that Rome might interrogate Will. So what? Those don't feel like high stakes. If Will can't die, all they can do is dissect him in some fashion, which has been done numerous times before.

If Will had a clear, *important* goal, such as stopping a global disaster from occurring, and the clock was ticking, and the opposition was breathing down his neck every step of the way to stop him (which is what we expect from thrillers), it would be a lot easier to craft those ten key scenes and put them in the right places.

You Need Conflict with High Stakes

This is why it's so critical that, when you start plotting out your novel, you hone that killer concept along with a clear, definitive goal for your protagonist along with the highest stakes possible. Conflict without stakes is impotent and lackluster. Readers will start falling asleep.

Third element missing: *some strong subplots, twists, or major complications*. There is no subplot to give the story depth. Because little happens, there's a lack of intriguing action. Maybe a lot of readers found the premise interesting enough to read the whole book, finding enjoyment in the tales of Will's relationships with famous people throughout the centuries. But to me, since all that is backstory (which clogs most of the pages), I got bored. I don't want to be *told* a story; I want to watch it happening.

I would have written this novel one of two ways. Either having Will on a clear, dangerous, vital mission (high stakes) that has the fate of the world in the balance or playing out Will's story in real time, starting with his life as Pilate's guard and hitting Jesus, with his goal of finding escape from his situation (and having that actually resolve at the climax).

The former, of course, would be better structurally because a novel that spans two thousand years as some epic biography would require a lot of rambling through one century after another. It would be hard to have a cast of characters unless those characters were also immortal.

If the author made it Will's goal to die (or be released of his curse, the same one that plagued Captain Jack Harkness in *Torchwood*), and he reached that goal at the climax through some epic, dangerous, high-stakes actions, that would be a viable and compelling goal. The Inciting Incident might, for example, be a scene in which Will discovers a possible solution to his problem, giving him hope—finally—that he might be released from his curse. What would proceed from there would be the progress amid obstacles that Will would make to reach his goal.

Do you see how a story framework like this would have a place for all the ten key scenes and would support a solid story? I do.

* * *

Your assignment: Brainstorm some ideas that take this basic story concept—about a man cursed by Jesus who's had to live centuries without dying—and turn it into a solid premise. Do what I did above: first **work on the goal** for the novel and imagine the climax scene in which he reaches or fails to reach his goal.

Think about **high stakes**. What kind of stakes could you create for this story that would be believable and tense? What actions could the opposition take that would imperil Will's goal in a huge way?

And finally, think about **character arc**. What could Will learn and experience that would ultimately change him? Give him the peace he yearns for (which could be dependent on his reaching the goal or not).

Try listing the ten key scenes once you've worked this all out. By now, from all these assignments, you should have these ten key scenes embedded in your brain!

Chapter 19: Conclusion

I always like to ask my best-selling author friends what methods they use to plot out their novels. Over the years, I've heard many diverse answers. It seems everyone has a method that they like and that works for them.

Some authors I know sit down to start writing a new novel with a general idea of the story they want to tell. They've come up with a few interesting characters, an intriguing situation, some bad guys or danger, and an idea of how the book will end. Then they dive in.

I know more than one author who writes a complete first draft, then throws it out and starts all over. One of these authors, who sells millions of copies of each of her novels, will go through three or four full drafts—all of which are tossed—before she writes "the keeper." She is stressed the entire time she is writing, worried whether she will come up with a good story in the end, and sweating over her looming deadline. She writes terrific novels, but I don't know why she puts herself through such agony. When I asked her why she doesn't first plot out her novels, she merely shrugged and said this was her process. She didn't seem all that eager to change, for, in the end, her novels always hit the tops of the best-seller lists.

Some authors I've questioned do take the time to plot. They'll come up with a list of a dozen or so scenes and feel confident enough to start writing their novel. But they go by feel, placing the scenes where they "fit best."

Sometimes the result from these methods is a well-crafted novel. Other times, not so much.

I'd like to posit that authors will have the *best* chance of ending up with a great novel if they use a method based on time-tested story structure.

We humans sometimes find change daunting. We like our comfortable patterns and habits. We may say, "Oh, I can't do that. That's just not me." I've heard a lot of excuses over the years from writers who say, "I just can't plot. It destroys my creativity" or "Plotting is too much work. It takes the joy out of the process. I just want to write."

I get all that—to a point. But, in most areas of life, we tend to look for the simplest and most practical way to accomplish something. Whether we're trying to repair a broken table, sew a dress, or train for a race, we don't want to waste a lot of time spinning our wheels and getting nowhere (unless we're on a stationary bike training for that race).

The simplest and most practical way to write a great novel is to use a method that eliminates guesswork—while still allowing for full creative expression.

Layering your novel may feel formulaic to you, but what's wrong with a formula? What's wrong with following a road map to get to your destination? A map might not be needed if you're just jogging to the corner market. But if you're trying to navigate through a complex terrain with myriad unmarked roads that lead to dead ends—like a rat maze—you'll save a lot of time and frustration by following the map.

I hope you'll give this layering method a try. Yes, it's a lot of front-end work, but I truly believe if you use this simple and practical method to laying out your story, you'll find, when you write "The End," that you've saved time and energy. And, more importantly, that you've enjoyed the process.

Writing should be fun, not a headache. When you can sit down at your computer, confident you have a solid framework figured out for your story, you won't suffer the worry and anxiety some of the biggest-selling authors go through day after day.

That's my hope for you and why I wrote this book. I want you to find joy in writing novels as you layer your way to success!

About the Author

C. S. Lakin is passionate about writing and helping writers see success in their writing journey. She's the author of twenty novels in various genres, which includes her seven-book fantasy series The Gates of Heaven and five novels in her historical Western romance Front Range series (under pen name Charlene Whitman). She works full-time as a copyeditor and writing coach.

Her award-winning blog for writers, Live Write Thrive, is an excellent resource for both fiction and nonfiction writers, with hundreds of posts on craft, marketing, and writing for life. She also puts out a newsletter to her readers with tips and insights on how to be productive and find success as a writer.

In addition to editing and proofreading, Lakin critiques more than two hundred manuscripts a year. If you've never had your work critiqued, you may be unaware of many weaknesses in your writing and story structure. Consider getting your scene outline or first chapters critiqued to help you see what needs work. You can learn more about her critique services at Critique My Manuscript.

Did you find this book helpful?
Please take a minute to leave an honest review on
Amazon!
It's the best way to say thank you to an author, and it
will help other writers.

Don't miss the books in The Writer's Toolbox series! These books cover nearly everything you need to know to write great fiction and structure solid stories!

Writing the Heart of Your Story: The Secret to Crafting an Unforgettable Novel

Shoot Your Novel: Cinematic Techniques to Supercharge Your Writing

The 12 Key Pillars of Novel Construction: Your Blueprint for Building a Solid Story

The 12 Key Pillars Workbook

5 Editors Tackle the 12 Fatal Flaws of Fiction Writing

Say What? The Fiction Writer's Handy Guide to Grammar, Punctuation, and Word Usage

Crank It Out! The Surefire Way to Become a Super-Productive Writer

Are you struggling with identifying the flaws in your writing? Take a look at the opening pages of *5 Editors Tackle the 12 Fatal Flaws of Fiction Writing:*

5 Editors Tackle the 12 Fatal Flaws of Fiction Writing

Introduction

Fiction writers often struggle to improve their craft. They want to write better, more effectively. Tell a stronger, more evocative story. But oftentimes what a writer envisions in her mind doesn't come across on the page.

The biggest challenge can come from the inability to see what *isn't* working. The prose feels off. The scene just isn't gelling. The dialogue sounds stilted or clunky. Writers consult their stack of reference books or jump online and search for answers on blog posts. They may even travel long distances to attend workshops and conferences to get to the heart of their problems.

But even then, the solutions are often elusive.

What writers need are not more books and instructors telling them what to do and how to do it. They need examples. And not just examples of great fiction writing. They need examples of weak, flawed writing too.

What helps writers most is to read passages that demonstrate flawed writing, then be shown revisions that target specific flaws and offer clear, effective solutions to those problems.

12 Fatal Flaws

When working on a manuscript, editors mark up and revise sections to show writing clients what's not working, why, and how these passages might be rewritten. We believe this is the best way to help writers identify their specific weaknesses, as well as learn how to get mastery over them.

Not every writer can afford to hire an editor to point out a manuscript's flaws. And wouldn't it be better for writers to arm themselves with the knowledge and skills needed to avoid succumbing to these writing flaws in the first place? We think so.

That's why we five editors put together a year-long course online—on the Live Write Thrive blog—specifically aimed at tackling the most problematic issues we see day in and day out as we edit and critique manuscripts. While there are undoubtedly more than twelve "fatal flaws" of fiction writing, we set out to examine in depth the most troublesome and ubiquitous of these.

We refer to these issues as fatal flaws because of their potential to cause "novel failure." Any one of these twelve flaws, if prevalent in a novel or other work of fiction, can be a writer's undoing. And because there is no one way to fix each flaw, we've created multiple examples to expose each one, using passages written in a variety of genres, points of view, and writing styles. We feel this wide assortment of more than sixty examples provides just the help writers need.

In addition to being editors, we are all novelists—who struggle with these fiction flaws like any other author. We hope that by sharing our decades of experience as writers as well as book editors, we might help you seek and destroy the fatal flaws in your writing.

How to Best Benefit from This Book

As you read each entry, try to identify what's wrong in the Before passage. Consider jotting down your observations in a notebook, paying special attention to the sections that apply most to your own writing issues. If you have a print copy, you may want to mark up these sections.

Pay attention to how the fatal flaw is presented and what solutions are offered to fix it. At the end of each chapter you'll find a checklist of the points covered—what you need to search for in your scenes or stories to ferret out the fatal flaw. You'll also get a bonus passage to work on, to help you test what you've learned (with a sample "correct" passage provided on the next page). We suggest you copy and print out these passages and work on them before peeking at the sample solution on the following page.

Every writer has a unique style and approach to fiction writing, so we hope that by reviewing a wide spectrum of examples, you will be able to spot potential weaknesses in your writing and fix them.

So as we tackle the twelve fatal flaws of fiction writing, jump in and take them on with us. If you're still having problems with specific flaws, consider hiring an editor with fiction-writing experience to help you home in on your weak areas and give you the skills to self-edit your work effectively. There's no reason any writer should have to experience novel failure.

So let's start tackling.

Fatal Flaw #1: Overwriting

Repetition. Redundancy. Useless words.

All fiction writers fall into the trap of overwriting. We're lured by the desire to be clear and thorough in our descriptions. To make sure the reader gets what we're trying to say. We think if we pack our sentences full of words, we'll get the point across. We'll convey the right emotion and, in turn, evoke the emotional response we long for in our readers.

But however logical that seems, the odd truth is that, more often than not, less is more. Plot and character motivation can come across more strongly and effectively with fewer words. Carefully chosen words. Just the right words put down just the right way.

We tend to underestimate our readers' ability to fill in blanks. We tend to get too close to what we are writing to see it clearly. We tend to doubt our own writing ability—and so we overwrite.

Gushing Is Fine . . . in a First Draft

Some writers find it helpful to gush onto the page in a first draft and worry about the cleanup later. Go ahead and do that. It's a good way to keep the creative juices flowing and get the story out in some form. But too often writers get attached to what they've written. The sentences harden into concrete seconds after they appear on the page or computer screen. It takes courage and stalwart determination to be a brutal self-editor and hack away at those sentences.

While some writers "underwrite" (a flaw we'll cover later in this book), most writers fall victim to overwriting. Overwriting is probably the most common flaw of fiction writing, and its tentacles reach into every aspect of a writer's story: narrative, dialogue, action, and internalizing. Like a contagion, it infects our scenes so they die a slow (or quick) death.

But good news! There is an antidote. The formula is one part determination, two parts knowledge, three parts diligence, and four parts mercilessness. Once you learn to detach emotionally from the words you write, the battle is half won.

Every word counts in your story. Every word has weight. It's heartbreaking to launch your story into a sea of readers and watching it sink before it clears the harbor. So before you break that bottle of champagne over the bow, learn to identify the symptoms of overwriting. Then, with cutlass in hand, hack away. The examples in this chapter will show you how.

The Forest for the Trees

When you put pen to paper, it's fully possible to underwrite. To fail to say what you meant to say. But just as possible, and more common, is *overwriting*—the tendency to say too much, in too many words, and crowd out the forest for the trees.

Overwriting takes many forms. Wordiness. Vagueness. Redundancy. Convolution. Pushing metaphors so far beyond the breaking point that they cease to be enlightening and become ridiculous instead.

In all forms, overwriting loses the forest for the trees. Readers get so snarled up in excessive words, tangled sentences, and overdone diction that the big picture is lost.

It's not fun to read. And often, it's not fun to write.

If your words feel forced or unnatural while you're writing them, you might be falling into this trap. It often happens when we try to "sound like real writers," or want to come across as particularly smart or poetic. In those cases we lose our own voices for something artificial.

Finding the Forest

You correct overwriting by letting go of your commitment to every individual tree, leaf, and branch and rediscovering the forest instead. Where's the heart of the scene? The point of the dialogue? The voice of the character?

Some say Michelangelo carved his famous *David* sculpture by chipping away everything that didn't look like David. That's how you cure overwriting.

See if you can catch the overwriting in this passage. What would you chip away?

Before:

As the sun was sinking down far below the edge of the purple, colorful horizon at the edge of the world, Jenny raised her wineglass to her ruby red lips and sighed sadly at seeing the day end. "It's over," she breathed.

Behind her, her impossibly handsome Italian boyfriend, Calvino, pushed his chair away from the table where they had been eating dinner like a panther slinking through the shadows of a dark night in Africa. She was just thinking he had been sitting there too long and wondered when he would come to join her by the edge of the expansive gold-rimmed balcony with its fluted decorations patterned after a famous architect from 1743.

He started to come toward her, and she waited for a long, interminable minute, staring at the purple sunset clouds, until he walked across the balcony, approached her shoulder, and bent down slightly so he could whisper in her ear. "It's never really over," he murmured.

Did this passage make you gag? It should have. Let's take a look at the revision.

After:

As the sun sank below the purple horizon, Jenny raised her wineglass to her lips and sighed at seeing the day end. "It's over."

Behind her, Calvino pushed his chair away from the dinner table. *It's about time,* she thought. She glimpsed his dark Italian features from the corner of her eye as he approached her on the gold-rimmed balcony.

"It's never really over," he whispered in her ear.

In this example, the edited version is far shorter—and more focused.

It cuts redundant language, so "As the sun was sinking down far below the edge of the purple, colorful horizon at the edge of the world" becomes "As the sun sank below the purple horizon."

It cuts a lot of the small in-between actions that can clutter prose: "She was thinking and wondering"; "he started to come toward her"; "he walked, approached, and bent down."

The rewritten version also implies the relationship between the two characters through their actions and words rather than explaining it outright. It cuts details that are irrelevant to the scene (the eighteenth-century architect) and a simile that, in the end, added nothing to the character or the moment.

By cutting all these examples of wordiness, we end up with a sharper scene—one that is focused on the forest. On the tension between the characters. On the lament over the end of the day and the promise of something more to come. Many a tree is gone, but the view is clearer.

Extrapolate that first example over the course of an entire scene, or an entire chapter, and you can see why overwriting can be such a problem—and why learning to cut back, *to focus on the scene you actually want your readers to see,* can go a long way toward creating a sharper, more vivid, and memorable story.

Want to read more? Get the Kindle ebook or paperback version on Amazon.com.

Made in the USA
Coppell, TX
06 March 2020